ARNOLD THE POET

ALSO BY THE SAME AUTHOR

Beauty, Truth and Humour—Essays (1924)
Thomas Hardy (third edition 1939)
The Quintessence of Bernard Shaw (second edition 1937)
The Way of Happiness: a Reading of Wordsworth (1948)
Walter de la Mare: a Study of his Poetry (1949)
Amphibian: a Reconsideration of Browning (1956)
The Novels and Plays of Charles Morgan (1959)

ARNOLD THE POET

by

HENRY CHARLES DUFFIN

NEW YORK

BARNES & NOBLE, INC.

PUBLISHERS · BOOKSELLERS · SINCE 1873

© Henry Charles Duffin 1962
First published in U.S.A.
by Barnes & Noble, Inc. 1963
Reprinted 1964

Printed in Great Britain by
Lowe & Brydone (Printers) Ltd, London

ONE MORE BOOK

FOR DOROTHY MY DELIGHT

Contents

Introduction

MY TITLE, like M. Bonnerot's,[1] stresses Arnold's function as a
poet. Garrod, writing in 1931, said that up to 1900 Arnold
was seen first as a critic and only then as a poet, and added that he
believed the last thirty years had reversed the order. It now appears,
from numerous recent publications, that attention has, since 1930,
gone back not so much to Arnold's criticism as to his other work in
prose, social, ethical and religious. This I should have thought was
the sphere in which he was least likely to achieve permanence, and
my hope is to revive critical interest in what I feel to be his most
important activity. In prose Arnold comes surely a long way after
Carlyle and Ruskin; in verse he stands as a close third to Tennyson
and Browning.

He indeed, like Coleridge, wrote much more prose than verse.
Nevertheless, I think Professor Willey is wrong in suggesting that
Arnold was a vital prose writer who dabbled in verse. Saintsbury
(still the final arbiter for me) judged that, though his poetic vein was
intermittent, his true greatness lay in poetry. Stopford Brooke said
that all that Coleridge did excellently in verse might be bound up
in twenty pages, but it should be bound in pure gold. The one
volume that comprehends the whole of Arnold's poetry is not a
large one, but it deserves binding in silver, at least.

The habit of comparing writers is not generally approved of, but
I have found it interesting, indeed inevitable, to bring Arnold at
various points into comparison with his two great contemporaries,
as well as sometimes with the elderly friend of his youth, Wordsworth. Arnold himself found such comparison natural. He wrote
to his mother in 1869: 'It might be fairly urged that I have less

---

[1] *Matthew Arnold: Poète*: by Louis Bonnerot, Paris, 1947.

poetical sentiment than Tennyson and less intellectual vigour and abundance than Browning—perhaps a fusion of the two—I am likely to have my turn.' Apart from the 'fusion' there is something in this, and it gives me my excuse.

Arnold is exceptional in being the only major poet to hold an exacting post during almost the whole of his writing-life. Chaucer and Spenser performed some light diplomatic duties, Shakespeare was a part-time actor, and Herrick—a country parson. Even Milton was Latin Secretary to the Commonwealth for only ten years out of a longer writing-life than Arnold's. But Arnold, from the age of twenty-nine to that of sixty-four, two years before he died, was an Inspector of Schools, and (apart from refusing to be punctual) carried out the continuous, laborious and not very congenial duties of the position with exemplary thoroughness. The additional duties, during ten years of that time, of Professor of Poetry at Oxford, he shouldered lightly, and if one visualises the amount of work he got through, in inspecting and papermarking, lecturing, travelling and writing, one is compelled to admit that this man, son of that equally energetic but shorter-lived Victorian, Arnold of Rugby, was, in one sense if not in others, something of a giant.

As a poet, he was neither giant nor god. Yet an unusually large proportion of his verse endures to be both admired and enjoyed, while very little is actually unreadable, other than (I suppose) *Merope*. The enjoyment is lasting but personal, not easily shared or communicated. I think I have contrived in the following pages to show reason why Arnold is worthy to be read and admired, but his peculiar quality, his special flavour, defies analysis, and has been, as I feared it might, impossible to 'get across'. I am also made very uncomfortable by the thought that I have had to begin by expressing great personal distaste for the morbid outlook of some of Arnold's poetry, but I hope the reader will be patient and read on to where I show the other side. It is simply not true to say, as Mr D. G. James says, that the poet was 'moved only to poetry in order to utter his grief and loss of hope'. He did win through to a more rational understanding of life and founded some of his greatest poems on it.

I must make it plain at once that my criticism, in this as in my earlier books, is based on the outmoded principle of seeking in my poet only the beauty and truth that are in him, and not extracting from him ideas I might wish him to have had. Chesterton[1] enunciated the modern approach clearly enough: 'The function of criticism can only be one function—that of dealing with the subconscious part of the author's mind which only the critic can express and not with the conscious part of the author's mind which the author himself can express.' Most modern criticism has taken this line, each critic reading into his author what meaning pleases him and the outlook of the moment. Mr Eliot roundly declares that the reader's interpretation, based perhaps on wider experience, may be better than the poet's own interpretation. This attractive but arrogant and dangerous doctrine has been refuted by Miss Helen Gardner in her book, *The Business of Criticism*, 1959: A poem, she says, is not what I choose to make of it. It is something which its author made with deliberation, choosing that it should say this and not that. . . . The power to recognise the poet's conception . . . and to read the poem in its light, is what I mean by true judgement in a critic.

This seems to me the sane and profitable line (advocated also by Hazlitt in his distant but not uncritical day), and it is the one I adopt. But whether what I find in Arnold comes from the upper or lower levels of his mind, I am not prepared, with M. Bonnerot, to applaud it for being 'well-adapted to the spiritual needs of our perplexed age'. Mr Kenneth Allott,[2] a practising member of this same 'perplexed age', finds Arnold 'congenial' and his sensibility 'modern'. But though it is not every poet, not even every great poet, that can be 'not for an age but for all time', we expect a major poet to have a more than parochial appeal. The 'perplexity' of the present age is based upon a narrow interpretation of circumstances so fantastic as to be patently ephemeral, and it is of only minor interest that the

---

[1] As quoted, and approved, by Mr Bernard Bergonzi in the *Critical Quarterly*, Vol. I, No. I, 1959.

[2] Whose excellent 'Penguin' selection, with a stimulating introduction, contains everything I want except *Urania*.

resulting state of mind coincides with the petulant mood of Arnold's earlier poetry. I have tried to judge his achievement from a standpoint, if not universal, at least less temporary than that chosen by a single fleeting 'age'.

(In quoting from or referring to another writer on Arnold I have not generally given the source in a footnote, but have left it to be inferred that the reference is to the book named in the bibliography.)

CHAPTER I

The Man and his Poetry

(a)

I SUPPOSE there never was a more perverse poem written than that one of Arnold's called *Growing Old*. Here was a man in his early forties—like Browning's lover, 'young, prosperous, sound and sane'. He had seen Wordsworth die at eighty, grieving over his recent loss but vigorous in body and mind; his mother was growing old gracefully at Fox How. Yet he sits down and indites a poem which I can only call a pitiful libel on life. It was doubtless written (in 1867) as a retort on *Rabbi Ben Ezra*, published in 1864, when Browning was fifty-two and so a little nearer, though not much nearer, to the period of life he is extolling than Arnold was when he intoned his dirge. Browning too erred in his estimate. Anyone who has had experience long enough and of the right quality knows that the 'last of life' is no more the 'best' than those years of 'angel infancy' which poets have sung, or the school-days which retired Colonels have proclaimed, as the happiest time of our life. Once you have achieved full self-consciousness, with mind and body fully developed—say just before or just after twenty—from then onwards proceed the 'best' decades of your life, as many as four, or even five if you are lucky and have been sensible.

But Arnold shuts his eyes to this, and hits out blindly at life. He not only analyses ruthlessly the defects of age—the loss of 'the glory of the form', the (not inevitable) foregoing of beauty, the decay of strength—but denies that there can be such a thing as mellowing and a thankful remembering of the great days; we must forget 'that we were ever young', let the dull realisation of change 'fester' in our heart, and 'spend long days' fretting over the late coming of recognition.

The poem would not be worth dissecting were it not that it is typical of a certain strain of thought in Arnold's poetry. The strain, one of bitterness and dissatisfaction, was a marked element in his mental make-up. No psychological reason for its presence can be adduced (and there is nothing pathological about it), except that his boyhood probably lacked that freedom which was so pleasingly abundant in Wordsworth's youth, and which I believe accounts for his genius for interpreting happiness. Garrod sees the trouble as resulting from disappointment in love—the failure of the Marguerite affair—but I cannot believe this. Whether he had been otherwise 'hurt in some vital part' in early life there is no means of knowing. The outward circumstances of his life were as good as those most poets have enjoyed.

As a boy Arnold was flippant and athletic, but achieved the English Poem Prize at Rugby. At Oxford he was idle and irresponsible, and won the Newdigate. At the age of twenty-five he fell in love with 'Marguerite', but at twenty-nine married the Frances Lucy of his more positive choice, had six children (accepting the early deaths of three of them with an admirable degree of stoicism) and a happy married life, though it is odd to notice how little mention his wife[1] gets in his family correspondence in comparison with his dachshunds (over which he was simply silly). Like Wordsworth he began writing (or publishing) late—the *Strayed Reveller* volume appearing when Arnold was twenty-seven, *Lyrical Ballads* when Wordsworth was twenty-eight—and though his first books did not sell they won a useful degree of recognition from 'those whose judgement is most valuable'. He was not uninterested in his work as an Inspector of Schools, though he said it was not—nor even lecturing at Oxford— 'the work for which he was born'. He found London society

---

[1] It would be irreverent to wonder what might have been the effect on Arnold and his poetry if he had married Marguerite. It would doubtless have been as disastrous as most people think a marriage between Wordsworth and Annette would have been.

stimulating, was, like Browning, a persistent diner-out (for the sake of the conversation), and enjoyed his membership of the Athenaeum, where he maintained his reputation as a wag.

If these circumstances offered obstacles to the growth of a poetic soul, there is nothing in them to suggest that Arnold ought to have been unhappy. And there is evidence to show that he was good and kind, as unhappy people seldom are. He does not seem to have been a 'Victorian parent' in any objectionable sense. An Inspector of Schools can be a figure of terror in his own world, but one of the teachers in his circuit said he was 'always patient and gentle with the children', on hearing which he commented, 'the great thing after all is humanity'; indeed it is clear that his whole purpose, as an educationist, was to humanise. People who met him found him kindly, courteous and tolerant, though he had an outward manner which caused the *D.N.B.* to voice a mild surprise at the proofs afforded by his letters of 'the extreme amiability of one generally set down as supercilious and sardonic'. Those letters, to his mother, sisters and wife, have been declared unreadable, but I find them good —affectionate, lively, informative (as in the account of his meeting with the King of Prussia). In the letters to Clough (of which we are fortunate to possess such an excellent edition, with a fascinating introduction, by H. F. Lowry) he is much less 'amiable', but still generous and true. His rich sense of humour (never seen in his poetry) once lost sight of decency (as humour may), when he speculated lightly on the possibility of his brother Tom having been drowned in a storm on the way to New Zealand—'which would be a pity, as he meant to enjoy himself there'. But it is a joy to think of him teaching a form at Rugby (as he did for a term or two after coming down from Oxford) and—at the news of a half-holiday brought round by a prefect—exclaiming, 'Well, thank God for that!' What relatives say is not always evidence, one way or the other, but his niece, Mrs Humphrey Ward, declared that it was exhilarating to be with him. 'Janeites' will be specially impressed by the family's opinion that Matthew was 'rather like Mr Woodhouse'.

It is quite clear that in Arnold's life there was no ground-bass of wretchedness such as we are aware of in the lives of Coleridge, Keats, Gissing. And yet the bitter element makes itself constantly felt at the core of his mind. From the age of twenty-five he seems to have been in a mood of permanent dejection (indeed this mood shows itself in the Rugby prize poem, though perhaps in 'mere Byronism'). At thirty he was wearying under the burden of life, complaining to Clough of growing old and life rushing away; he himself has 'dawdled life away, and all is over'. The times are 'arid'—there are no great figures to enrich the English scene: this in an age that produced Thomas Arnold, Ruskin, Browning, Dickens, Carlyle, Tennyson, Newman, Jowett, Mill, Darwin, Huxley, Peel, Gladstone, Shaftesbury, George Eliot, Florence Nightingale. . . . It is true that all these men and women have only attained their full stature in perspective, so that it is our own age that appears comparatively unheroic. But a man of Arnold's quality should not have been completely blind to the virtues of his contemporaries. The blindness showed itself especially with regard to the other poets of his time. Great critic as he was (and surely a critic's powers should not fall flat when confronted with contemporary work), there is no single fellow-poet of whom he had much to say in the way of appreciation. Of Clough more later, but Arnold's refusal to see anything in the *Bothie* was merely wilful (Browning revelled in the splendid sprawling poem). Tennyson 'trifled with poetry', was 'deficient in intellectual power', and was 'not a great spirit'. Browning had, at one time, 'only a moderate gift', but later proved to be the only contemporary poet in whom Arnold was willing to recognise 'a real man of genius'. The letters between Arnold and Browning published by John Drinkwater in the *Cornhill* for December 1913 show that they were on very cordial terms. Earlier poets too were belittled, other than Shakespeare, Milton and Wordsworth (and even Shakespeare was less than Homer because less 'perfect'). His querulous criticisms of Keats were corrected by the later essay, but he thought Shelley's prose would outlive his verse and complained that Chaucer lacked high seriousness. Contemporary prose suffered the same denigration, and it might seem that the faculty of admiration—a normal concomitant of greatness—had gone sour in Arnold under the working of his general disgruntlement.

In the matter of the general situation his despondency did not lack grounds. In the forties and fifties of the nineteenth century England was not, to an observer of wide sensibility, the pleasant place to live in that it afterwards became. The disgrace of the owner-ship of slaves abroad was not yet forgotten, and at home, though the iniquitous penal code had been eased it was still harsh, and inhuman conditions of labour, both child and adult, had been but slightly ameliorated by the early Factory and Mines Acts. An appalling degree of poverty was widespread, and was callously regarded, as in the case noted by Arnold of the poor girl Wragg. Elementary educa-tion was scanty, and was often administered in hideous and inadequate buildings. The result was the existence of a teeming populace of degraded habits and instincts who, in London and other large towns, lived—by the grace of the slum-landlords, often in cellars and always without sanitation—on the back-door steps of their civilised fellow-citizens, so that to go down among the dog-stealers of the Wimpole Street area, as Elizabeth Barrett did in 1846, was a terrifying adventure. When, in 1849, Arnold, probably writing in a temper (he was in the middle of the Marguerite entanglement), told Clough they were living in damned times, he added some other items that infuriated him, such as newspapers and cities, as well as the 'absence of great natures' already refuted. He included a complaint that the world was becoming more comfortable for 'the mass' (he cannot have meant the mass of manual workers) and less comfortable for 'those of gift and distinction', which continues to be the grouse of the gifted and distinguished a century later.

His mental condition (which might well have been simple anger but reads like despair) has been partly attributed to the estrangement from Clough, and it does seem that as these two brilliant young men, friends not at Rugby but earlier and at Oriel, developed they dis-closed a tendency to rub each other the wrong way (as did Lamb and Coleridge, and doubtless David and Jonathan). Arnold's coldness towards Clough's poems was, as we have seen, a facet of his general attitude to contemporary poetry, but it was unnecessary to tell his friend in a letter that to hear other men praising the *Bothie* maddened him and made him feel inclined to 'dispense with' Clough himself. Clough, on his part, was luke-warm and patronising in an article he wrote on Arnold's poetry for the *North American Review* in 1853. But Arnold not only took this good-naturedly, but continued to insist that it was Clough's judgement on his poetry that he valued most. When Clough was trying to get a post Arnold wrote, 'Make use of me as if I were your brother', and his last letter, shortly before Clough's death, ended, 'God bless you!'

I think the differences with Clough constituted but a drop in the salt ocean of Arnold's mood. Perhaps initially responsible was his early absorption of Senancour's feeble philosophy with its renunciation of will and responsibility, resulting in a backboneless ennui. That a man of Arnold's calibre should have been so uncritically attracted is surprising, but we all know what effect a seductive writer can have on the mind of a thinking man before it has been matured by experience; and when the reversal of outlook came, as it was bound to, we shall find it marked in the difference between *Obermann* and *Obermann Once More*. And there is that matter of experience. Froude, writing in 1849, said Arnold had 'never known the shady side of life', and since his life was spent between Oxford, Fox How and the Board of Education his experience could not but be limited. But experience is only the material on which the mind works, and an imaginative mind can do more with a few fragments of experience than a dull one with a whole world. If despair was the medium of Arnold's contact with life, it might only have been intensified by a wider experience in these early middle decades. One must give him credit for genuine feelings of unrest and dissatisfaction with the thing he did have full experience of—the English way of life among the middle classes. Yet Trevelyan says the period was marked by interest in religious questions, seriousness of thought and self-discipline of character, and a great artist should be at least on a level with the best contemporary philosophy.

The outlook was superficial, and gives rise to the suspicion that

Arnold's intellect was not of the strongest. J. C. Shairp was out-spoken in his condemnation of such a 'false and uninteresting view of life', and told Clough he thought blank dejection was not worth 'setting to music'. Arnold himself felt a 'want of intellectual robust-ness', a 'languor of spirit'. He was oppressed by the intensifying conflict of science and religion—though in the mid-nineteenth century there was at least a conflict, and on equal terms, not the David and Goliath affair it has become, with David not too handy with the sling and nothing in his pocket but some small potatoes.

And there was in Arnold a more serious deficiency still. Charles Morgan said that though the appearance of life may be meaningless the reality is quite other: there *is* order and significance, and not to see this is impious and mad. We need not suppose that Arnold was as deep in as this. Professor Willey asserts that to Arnold life had momentous meaning, and certainly he did not carry despair as far as the 'beatnik' of today, who gives up because he sees man in the grip of uncontrollable forces, whereas Arnold did at least believe the 'strange disease' was curable by the will to live. But as yet he derived no help from spiritual faith. At the time when all but the 1867 poems were being written, while he was still under forty, his hold on religion was not firm enough to provide any sort of shield against pessimism. Like Clough, he had been brought up to Angli-canism, and like Clough he had abandoned orthodox theology. Nor, at this time, had he learnt to value the mystic approach, if we can judge by his reference to 'mystics and such cattle'. He quotes, with seeming approval, a statement by his adored Goethe that Homer had taught him that life was Hell, but neglects to note Goethe's 'reflection' that 'to recognise God where and howsoever He may reveal Himself is the only true bliss on earth'. Arnold was, as yet, without the 'consolations of philosophy' in any exalted form.

(b)

The poetical reflection of all this ingrained sourness is the volumes of 1849, 1852 and 1855, with some accretions from the editions of

1853, 1854 and 1857—that is, in the poems written before Arnold was
thirty-five. The title-poem of his first volume, *The Strayed Reveller*,
is a light preliminary to what was to come. It is indeed a young
man's poem, with a dance in its heart, both of form and feeling, which
its author never recaptured. The vision of life it offers is nicely
balanced, and the poet, the youth, being given the last word, comes
nearer than Arnold afterwards came to the gospel of joy that is the
poet's true heritage.

But after this we are enveloped in gloom, with but a very few
star-holes. Life is such 'fierce work' that one would rather die than
go through it again; is indeed 'hardly worth the pain of birth'. Life
consists of a struggle with passions, except for 'milder natures'
like Fausta (so Wordsworth had exempted *his* sister from the
dutiful repression called for by the stern daughter of the voice of
God). Even in the 'placid and continuous whole' of nature the poet
with his 'sad lucidity of soul' can find peace and patience but no joy.
The Prelude, with its vision of

> the deep enthusiastic joy,
> The rapture of the Hallelujah sent
> From all that breathes and is,

was not yet published, but later Arnold was to extol the 'power
with which Wordsworth feels the joy offered to us in nature'.
Meanwhile in *Mycerinus* he gave an over-sympathetic handling to
the unstoical and resentful king, turning his back on life, and went
on to complain that his own well-favoured life was 'one long
funeral'. It is possible that the poem, *The Question*, in which this
astonishing description is offered was a mere exercise in melancholy,
written for an admiring if wondering sister; the fact that Arnold
did not reprint the poem till 1877 rather suggests that he
realised the enormity. But his mind was at this period orientated
to gloom. He cannot see a gipsy child without thinking of
nectarous poppies and grey-haired kings who loathed life. Even
the great sonnet on Shakespeare glories in the dramatist's voicing
of pain, weakness and grief, and overlooks the happiness of

Ferdinand and Miranda, the love of Beatrice and Benedick, the gladness of Portia and the gaiety of Rosalind—all of which are equally well 'voiced'.

I am—only too obviously—ignoring the beauty and force that went to the creation of these poems, and doubtless over-much regretting that all the pellucid art should have been devoted to the dark. However, that was Arnold's mood: the 'vague dejection' that weighed down his soul was a chronic condition. Even love could not rouse him. He is a little too old and much too sophisticated to enjoy a first love-affair, and feels painfully helpless in 'Time's current strong'. In spite of Marguerite's allure he derives no real happiness from his encounters with her, and his most passionate desire is to be alone on the snowy peaks. His own sense of isolation he must erect into a general truth of human nature—of how all men are 'enisled' in the sea of life. To some extent this is undeniable, but since, as he admits, the nightingales sing across the water, the situation is far from intolerable. Even the recalling of an intensely happy moment, when Marguerite's 'unforgotten voice', with its lute-like, melancholy tones, had thrilled his heart, now comes back to him 'anxiously and painfully', 'drearily and doubtfully'.

Sometimes what he writes reads like a parody of an attitude. Youth, with its 'hurrying fever', has been a 'hated time', and youth and age have only one feature in common—discontent. A few people are briefly happy, but if fate, by a 'weak indulgence', prolonged their happiness, this would mean the prolonging of unhappiness for others. Happy thoughts may (doubtfully) brighten life for some, but—says the poet—they 'never shone for me'. His analogy for a sight that displeases him is 'repellent as the world'.

The 1852 volume finds him still envying the happiness of the birds, for man's lot is to know that

> Peace has left the upper world
> And now keeps only in the grave.

Lyrically he mourns for Wordsworth, but lapses into one of his
false generalisations:

> So it is, so it will be for aye,
> Nature is fresh as of old,
> Is lovely, a mortal is dead.

If he had got out of his boat on Rydal and gone and looked at a
child he would have seen that mankind too is lovely, fresh and
immortal, just like nature, renewing itself in the same way and to
better purpose. His typical 'pair' is two people who from the
sunshine of life have grown to be old, blind, lamenting their faded
and ignoble lives.

It was now that Arnold threw off that cheery little poem called
Destiny, in which 'the Powers that sport with man' (one remembers
how their President 'sported' with Tess) are invoked, and man is
defined as 'an aimless unallayed Desire'—which might be a scientific
description of an amoeba. The poem was not reprinted. One can
imagine Arnold chuckling at the terms of his vitriolic epigram but
deciding that it went beyond the rules of classical restraint.

Empedocles upon Etna itself, title-poem and longest in the 1852
volume, expresses a worthier view of life. Empedocles is no coward
soul (as I am tempted to call Arnold). His message to Pausanias is—
not to despair: life teems with ill but provides scope for man's
efforts. In the later soliloquy he admits that his discontents are due
to his having lived too long and lost touch with the new age—he
makes his exit violently but almost with joy. There are a few more
signs here that Arnold could write poetry other than when the black
dog was on his back. One of these poems, *The Buried Life*, closes
with the suggestion that love may bring not only peace but the
certainty for which he pined. Like Coleridge, Arnold failed to find
the absolute in either love or poetic inspiration, and, glimpsing it
here, he feels that such experiences are too rare. Yet a single lamp
will light up a dark room, and if he had been a wiser man he would
have allowed these 'hours of insight' more weight. He might have
been able to put into practice the truth he professed to have found in

Wordsworth—that when confronted by the 'cloud of mortal destiny' the poet's cue is to 'put it by'. The only poem in this volume where he seems to have done this is that most tranquil of all his poems, *The Future*.

The few poems added during the years 1853-7 continue the dejected strain. The beautiful *Requiescat* (a companion piece to Landor's *Rose Aylmer* and Browning's *Evelyn Hope*) must needs add to the lament for the girl the morbid note of self-pity—

> In quiet she reposes—
> Ah! would that I did too.

Haworth Churchyard celebrates frustrated hope and the untimely death of genius. The two long narratives, for all their glory of heroes, are in essence cheerless: one showing the triumph of cunning evil, the other the grief and loss that come of folly and blind error. And the *Stanzas from the Grande Chartreuse* not only present an exacerbated picture of the poet's dismal state of mind but offer as explanation that he is (like Empedocles) out of sympathy with his age—

> Wandering between two worlds, one dead,
> The other powerless to be born.

The *Obermann* stanzas and *The Scholar Gipsy* I shall speak about presently, as they provide a jumping-off ground towards Arnold's second period.

What I have been saying was perhaps put more succinctly by Clutton-Brock when he said that Arnold's bursts of 'divine poetry' come unexpectedly, like a beautiful voice heard suddenly singing in a lecture-room. This is severe. A kinder comparison might be the musical parts of a church service. I have doubtless nagged excessively, and must ask forgiveness, but Arnold's personal state of mind, accentuated by his fear of the tempo and uncertainty of the age, produced far too much of what has been called a 'melodious whine'. His mood had brightened, and the age itself had grown less disturbing, before he published the *New Poems* of 1867. One must give him credit for sticking to his point, and learning from experience when it came.

(c)

In the 'sixties the condition of England, though still deplorable by the standards of the 'welfare state', was sufficiently improved to provide hope that things would go on getting better. The nation seemed to be progressing towards the attainment of its two ideals, prosperity and peace. The spectacle of poverty became a shade less appalling as the lot of wage-earners in town and country improved. The middle classes showed signs, in Arnold's eyes, of a possible transformation, through the spread of culture, to a serious and instructed ruling order. He saw them 'slowly awakening from their intellectual sleep'. He felt that, although belief in the supernatural, Christianity itself, was passing away, since the English were unaware of this it left them unaffected. He felt he could at least admire his times as 'a critical age'.

This external amelioration, however, was not marked enough to have brightened Arnold's melancholy philosophy if there had not been also independent temperamental changes. In spite of the deaths of his three sons his domestic happiness seems to have grown deeper: the fulcrum of domestic happiness is the relation between husband and wife, and it is only in the later letters to Fanny Lucy[1] that Arnold becomes demonstratively affectionate. There are signs that his mind is coming to appreciate joyous things: he is 'getting to like Ruskin' and finding the beginning of a New Year 'very animating'. He reads 'five pages of the Greek Anthology every day, looking out all the words I do not know: this is what I shall always understand by education'. Narrow, perhaps, but delightful, and smacking of a certain zest for life.

The primary ground for the brighter spirits is the entering upon new and exhilarating forms of activity, with wider recognition. In 1857 he was for the first time given work commensurate with his quality, on his appointment to the Oxford Professorship of Poetry. (He had started with two instincts, to write poetry and to teach.)

---

[1] I cannot like 'Flu', though it is better than 'Ba', and has the advantage of being immediately pronounceable.

Though he had been given the Professorship on the strength of his poetry, now, for the time being, he dropped poetry for prose, turning first to criticism, where he felt his power and was soon acknowledged as a great critic. His influence, exerted through his essays and lectures, was very great, and knowing this inspired and cheered him. He spoke in his letters of his satisfaction at 'the hold among these younger men what I write has taken'. This led to a popularisation of his poetry, and he expressed surprise at finding that the public knew and cared for it. In the province of education, too, his voice was beginning to tell. Though still only an Inspector of Schools he was encouraged by his superiors to put forward his views. He framed high conceptions of State education, which he was urging long before his brother-in-law persuaded Parliament to adopt it—in a sadly imperfect form.

There was a third sphere where his influence became marked, bringing him again much gratification—the sphere of morals and religion. Like other intellectual young men, Arnold had cut adrift from religious belief, but in his forties he set his hand to the work of examining dogmatic theology with a view to discovering the true grounds of faith. This was congenial work, for, if one can judge from his notebooks (after 1860), Arnold was, next to Coleridge, the most religious-minded poet of the century. Moreover, as he went on, and published his results, he believed he was propagating the religion of joy. Yet religion was to him an abstract thing. He had no experience that could give him a strong personal sense of God: all he could do for his readers—and they were many, and they thought it was much—was to assemble the good elements in life and claim that they represented God. It is an approach, certainly, and a logical approach, and perhaps the one along which his audience was most likely to be led. He never became an orthodox Christian, but valued the joyous Greek element in Christianity more than the stern Hebraic.

He saw and proclaimed the enormous importance of morality, but here he took a different line. The morality he inculcated was the Goethean-Carlylean morality of renunciation and repression,

based on the assumption that man's impulses are mainly bad. (At this
same time Ruskin was teaching that right action was not what you
compelled yourself to do against your inclination, but that a deed
was not good unless you enjoyed doing it: 'Taste is the only
morality'.) Especially in sex Arnold considered repression necessary
—and a hundred years later we have seen repression lifted and the
licentiousness and promiscuity that have resulted. Nevertheless, he
urged the necessity for a sense of joy in life, and no one teaches this
without knowing it himself. Not only were his ideals more kindly,
but he shows pleasure in their promulgation. His mood in poetry
had been querulous; in prose he is serene and detached.

But, says Trilling, 'as he went forward to cheerfulness his poetry
died'. There have been other explanations of this (only partial)
death. Raleigh thought that 'in a sense the critic in Arnold killed the
poet'. Kingsmill declares that the poet disintegrated into the prophet.
Others say that you cannot be an Inspector of Schools and remain a
poet. Some, looking further back, assert that poetry died with
dandyism. No 'explanation' is, as a matter of fact, necessary beyond
the simple action of time. Arnold continued to write poetry, and
excellent poetry, till he was forty-five, and very few English poets—
I believe only Chaucer, Milton, Cowper and de la Mare—have
added to their reputation after that age. Arnold told his mother in
1861 that he proposed to 'give the next ten years earnestly to poetry'.
In the event he published the volume of 1867, containing some of the
most memorable poems of the century, most of them reflecting the
change that had come over his outlook on life.

(d)

Let me first clear away certain poems obstructive to my purpose,
my purpose of showing that the *New Poems* are more hopeful in
mood than the earlier volumes. *Growing Old* I have spoken of: it
was perhaps not meant seriously, and it is counterbalanced—its
acidity neutralised—by two milder poems on death, *A Wish* and
The Last Word. In the former Arnold pictures himself letting his

spirit go, refreshed and ennobled by the beauty of the natural scene; in the other, bitter as it is, he at least sees the human spirit going out heroically. The most striking contrast with the general mood of the *New Poems* is afforded by *Dover Beach*, and I am thankful to have Messrs Tinker and Lowry's assurance that this great but despondent poem is a hollow echo from the earlier world, having been composed in 1850. I shall look more closely at it presently.

To realise how plainly night has yielded to day one has only to read the *Obermann* poem of 1849 (published in 1852) and follow it with *Obermann Once More*, published in 1867. The earlier poem was written entirely in the minor key. Arnold put aside Wordsworth's calm and Goethe's strength in favour of Senancour's backboneless conception of a cold world and a hopelessly tangled age, where we are in the grip of 'some unknown Power'. Under a stern Alpine sky Arnold saluted the unstrung will and broken heart. Now, years later, he conceives the once despairing philosopher as insisting that a new hope must spring and the world be made anew by 'thought and joy'. It is nothing less than the return of health after long illness.

The same mellowing of spirit is discernible in those twin (but not identical twin) poems, *The Scholar Gipsy* (1853) and *Thyrsis* (1867). The thought that underlay Arnold's presentation of the immortal wanderer was that the living world was fit only to be shunned, that modern life was in itself a 'strange disease' which would infect the free spirit with doubt and despair. But in the new poem it is Thyrsis who is reproved for despairing too quickly and turning his back on the world, while Corydon stays to greet with joy the Thames-side flowers and with confidence the sight of the Tree yet crowning the hill to prove that the Scholar, emblem of hope and youth, has *not* fled like the Tyrian trader.

So too with *Rugby Chapel*. Whatever Thomas Arnold may be in the eyes of Lytton Strachey, Mr Hugh Kingsmill and Sir Harold Nicolson, to those who knew him he was the greatest of men, and to his son Matthew fifteen years after his death a light shining in darkness. Through the Headmaster the almost cynical poet is

inspired to believe in the possible greatness of man and to see the
race marching on—

> On to the bound of the waste,
> On to the City of God.

Browning himself wrote no more fervent *sursum corda*. Indeed,
among the sonnets of this volume is one, *Immortality*, in which
Arnold beats Browning at his own game, not only showing the
worker on earth continuing to 'strive and thrive' in the after-life,
but showing also that Browning's creed of a better world to com-
pensate for the ills of this one will not work. Immortality will be no
consolation prize for earthly suffering, but something achieved by
those who have advanced with well-knit souls. This is to put
depression in its place.

A Southern Night is sad with the memories of his dead brother and
sister-in-law, but rejoices in their gentleness and nobility of soul
that proclaimed them allied to the divine. Here too is *Calais Sands*,
the one love poem where Arnold is not in a fume and fret with
himself, or the beloved, or the world, or life, or 'a God, a God',
but just tenderly in love. And that admirably argued 'epilogue' to the
Laocoon is written in a glory of enthusiasm for his own art of poetry:

> No painter yet hath such a way,
> Nor no musician made, as they,
> And gathered on immortal knolls
> Such lovely flowers for cheering souls.
> Beethoven, Raphael cannot reach
> The charm which Homer, Shakespeare teach.

Perhaps before all is the poem, *Palladium*, that perfect rendering
of the exalted function of man's deathless spirit:

> Still doth the soul, from its lone fastness high,
> Upon our life a ruling effluence send;
> And when it fails, fight as we will, we die;
> And while it lasts, we cannot wholly end.

There is every evidence that Arnold had learnt, in these middle
years, to 'possess his soul', and that he had come, as all but the most

foolish and obstinate come, to 'accept the universe'. He now knew that life was not a matter for peevish complaint but a great gift, worthy of praise and with infinite possibilities, and that poetry was a means to the good life.

(e)

It is not to be supposed that the intellectual content of Arnold's poetry is nothing more than an expression of disgruntlement in the earlier volumes and acceptance in the later. The poems teem with thought of a more interesting kind. Not that the intellectual content of poetry is as important as Arnold tried, in the Preface of 1853, to persuade himself it was, or that he is a profound thinker. His thinking, in criticism and sociology, is sometimes confused and prejudiced. But ideas that have been intensely felt (like those of Hamlet's soliloquies) may form the proper stuff of poetry, and an examination of some of these in Arnold may help us to see the man in his poetry.

His general attitude to life was more serious and less temperamental than the feelings of dejection changing to complacency that have been so far depicted. He never achieved anything so constructive as optimism. His tendency is to suggest that the best we can hope to reach is a state of calm. He holds up for 'Fausta's' admiration his conception of

> The general life, which does not cease,
> Whose secret is not joy but peace,

though he had already admitted that 'Calm's not life's crown'. He claims too that the calm of death is not what we are born for: there is, within our legitimate grasp, 'a bliss on this side death'. He learns from 'Euphrosyne' that there are people blest from birth to know 'a bliss within' that shines from them like a radiance, so that they bring joy to their fellows (this is Wordsworth's *Happy Warrior*). The message of *Early Death and Fame* is '*live* while you are young, so that if death should come untimely you may feel, *I have lived*'. In short, it seems that Arnold's attitude to life might after all be

found in those lines which come so surprisingly at the death of
Sohrab:

> Unwillingly the spirit fled away,
> Regretting the warm mansion which it left,
> And youth, and bloom, and this delightful world.

Gray had said it perfectly, but this is beautifully said too.

Arnold is not always so definite, but at least he knows that life is
an amalgam, so that time

> Brings round to all men
> Some undimmed hours.

We have seen how he allowed, just once, the young dreamer, the
strayed reveller, to look beyond both the superficial and the dismal
view of life to the sheer joy of living. And once he takes the forward
vision of *The Future*, with life itself becoming more and more deeply
tinctured with the immortality which is its end.

So much for life, the life of man. What of man himself? Whether
Arnold judged human nature subjectively or from observation, his
conclusions are not favourable. Most men, for him, live meaningless
lives in a brazen prison, and the few that escape behave with complete
irresponsibility and come to wreck. Is there no life, the poet asks,
but these alone?

> Madman or slave, must man be one?

He gives thanks that there are other possibilities, but he will not
recognise the existence of a third class of sane workers and inspired
thinkers. Why should he suppose himself unique?—or did he feel
himself a slave in a brazen prison? In *Rugby Chapel* he is willing to
admit that though most men live wasted lives and die forgotten,
some strive after an ideal that is fruitful and memorable, but even
these would fall by the wayside unless upheld by strong souls like
his father, through whom he can at least believe that there were men
of the past, great and good, servants and sons of God.

Man is a duality, with an outward behaviour frivolous and futile,
hiding a 'genuine self' of true value. And there is in man a deep

desire to become acquainted with this 'buried life', but his delvings, being unsuccessful, bring him nothing but sadness. Not only is there this division of the individual, but each man is divided from his fellows by a certain isolation, and this not only because each 'mortal' is by nature an 'island' but through deliberate concealment of the self from others for fear of inviting indifference or contempt.

The salve for at least some of these pains and penalties of human nature is love. Outside the score or so of personal love-poems, love plays no great part in Arnold's poetry—a far less vital part than in any other of the 'romantics' from Wordsworth to Browning. Arnold's one great presentation of a love-story is *Tristram and Iseult*, and it seems that he was drawn, like others, to the deathless theme by interests other than love. Yet he does, once or twice, give love its true place. He tells Marguerite that though he shares the admiration women have for heroic qualities in man—force and will and fearless-ness—she must learn that the rare and precious thing is love, and that the Creator's will is that men and women shall be 'gentle, tranquil, true'. More significantly, perhaps, after telling us, in *The Buried Life*, how completely the truth about ourselves and our life is hidden from us he says,

> Only—but this is rare—
> When a beloved hand is laid in ours,
> A bolt is shot back somewhere in our breast . . .
> And then (man) thinks he knows
> The hills where his life rose
> And the sea where he goes.

Objection has been taken to the word 'thinks', which is said to invalidate the knowledge come at through love. But I do not believe Arnold meant this. We cannot *know* anything certainly, and to 'think' we understand the mystery of life is to exchange doubt for peace. It was as a poet that Arnold discovered this great imaginative truth. Wordsworth had declared, nearly half a century earlier,

> By love . . . all grandeur comes,
> All truth and beauty, from pervading love;

and nearly a hundred years later de la Mare spoke again:

> Only love can redeem
> This truth, that delight . . .
> Restore to the lost the found,
> To the blinded sight.

It is distressing that Arnold should have lapsed from this funda-
mental faith, to the extent of denying the very existence of love
even in the very act of invoking it for himself:

> Ah, love, let us be true
> To one another! for the world . . .
> Hath really neither joy nor love . . .

How is it possible for a poet, for the sake of a mood, to sully his
poetry with an untruth so obvious and so unworthy!

Parallel with his slight treatment of love is an exiguous presentation of woman. There is the wraith-like figure of Marguerite, the
passion-drenched first Iseult and the meek and tender Iseult of
Brittany. There are hints of a pleasant sister-relation with 'Fausta'
and of the lovely personality of a sister-in-law; others of a tender
love for his wife, and of grief for the girl whose death called forth
Requiescat. The only formulated opinion of women is given in the
third *Switzerland* poem, where women are called 'things that live
and move Mined by the fever of the soul', and longing for a strong
ruthless man to come along and rule them. The picture is not
improved by the observations in *Haworth Churchyard*, and it is not
till quite late that the noble figure of Merope comes to redress the
balance. All the other 'romantics' do better than Arnold in this
matter, but in addition to the few examples of female portraiture
there is a measure of theory, amounting to what might be called
feminism, offered in *Urania*, which will be looked into presently.
The spirit of the poem is that of Henry Cust's *Non Nobis* and
Humbert Wolfe's *Uncommon Woman*, and if it can be taken to
represent more than a passing phase of thought, moves Arnold
some stages up the list of poets who have written nobly of woman.

One of the odd things about Arnold's presentation of human nature is the way in which he tries to excuse its weaknesses—especially those he discovers in himself—by attributing them to the action of a 'God' or a 'Power'. The best known, indeed amusing, instance occurs in the very first of the *Switzerland* poems. For the second year he meets Marguerite at Thun, and, smitten by her charm, is about to propose marriage, but thinks again—'Better not, perhaps.' This prudential restraint does not, according to Arnold, arise in his own mind but comes from without and above:

> in tones of ire
> I hear a God's tremendous voice,
> 'Be counselled, and retire!'

To us this might seem a disproportionate use of force; to Mr Kingsmill it will be merely the ghostly wagging of Papa's admonitory finger. To Arnold it may have been no more than a metaphor.

Later in the same series, pained by his inability to get into sympathetic contact with a mind and personality so alien as Marguerite's, he first elevates this personal factor into a general statement that all people are similarly cut off from each other, like islands in the sea, and then calls in some external power for explanation—

> A God, a God their severance ruled.

In *The Buried Life* he uses the conventional word 'fate' to account for similar difficulties of communication. Elsewhere, conscious of his failure to make the best use of his talents, he assumes a 'Power beyond our seeing', and invents an odd theory of a past existence where gifts were badly distributed—another attempt to evade responsibility for personal weakness. In *Obermann* this 'Power' again exercises a thwarting effect:

> We, in some unknown Power's employ,
> Move on a rigorous line;
> Can neither, when we will, enjoy,
> Nor, when we will, resign.

C

Once, with yet more pagan effect, the Power is pluralised—

> chartered by some unknown Powers
> We stem across the sea of light by night.

Just a picturesque form of fatalism, doubtless. All the references are
to the period of his religious doldrums, and it is merely surprising
that a man of his mental calibre should, for a time and in his own
fashion, have shared in the common habit of attributing life's ills
and the stupidities of human nature to 'the devil' or the stars.

Arnold had no pervading sense of God—'God and the immortality
of life, Beneath all being evermore to be' (quoted by Helen Darbi-
shire from one of the Dove Cottage notebooks)—and the mystical
faculty was less well developed in him than in either Tennyson or
Browning. Nevertheless, before he got bogged down in his religion
of ethics there are signs that he knew what it meant to have intuitions
of ultimate beauty and truth. I have already quoted from *The
Buried Life* to show his realisation that one such glimpse may come
through human love, and from *A Summer Night* to show a further
glimpse founding itself on the divine possibilities of human personality. He arrives at an original if questionable conception in *Morality*.
He has contrasted the laborious life of man with the effortless
workings of Nature. Then he makes Nature say that before the
emergence of what we call the space-time continuum she, herself
so carefree now, was aware of a severity and earnestness in her great
original, God. It would seem that a serious intention in the '*logos*'
resulted in a dichotomy, gaiety in nature and gloom in man (both
as seen by Arnold).

The most interesting of these poems concerned with Arnold's
sense of God is the early one called *In Utrumque Paratus*. The philosophical title suggests a complete absence of such sense, but the first
stanza contains a vision of creation which could only have been
attained by a mind sensitive to the wonder of that inconceivable event.
Arnold sees the 'sacred world' form itself silently in the imagination of
God, the all-pure, and presently, 'a long-mused thought', taking shape
in form and colour. Man can enter into the 'coloured dream' of God

only by achieving a 'lonely pureness' himself—a not unworthy description of the mystic experience and its preliminaries. He goes on to admit that the universe may have had no such numinous origin, but may be a product of the interaction of material forces, with man not part of God's dream but the sole dreamer.[1]

Of the soul, the mind in its divine aspect, the point of contact between man and God, Arnold has little to say, but we have seen how, in the brilliant poem *Palladium*, he presents a high conception of the soul. In the earlier poem, *Self-Dependence*, he had identified the soul with the self, and had decided that only by living as undistracted as the stars of heaven can man be himself and possess his soul. This leads into the quietism which is, poetically, Arnold's ideal. He, like the world, has chosen the path of work, action, success, but feels the attraction of the contemplative life. *Bacchanalia*, under all its lavishness of detail, presents the beauty of spiritual quiet. Wordsworth, in the *Memorial Verses* and in *Obermann I*, is made to adopt the philosophy of quietism, achieving 'sweet calm' by 'putting by the cloud of mortal destiny' and 'averting his ken from half of human fate'. The analysis of Wordsworth's mental attitude is inaccurate, and he was certainly not a quietist: the circumstances of his life, like those of Arnold's, afforded small scope for the cultivation of the quietist ideal, which, as Garrod (calling it 'the dedicated life') says, is perhaps not essential to poetry—'What dedicated life had Shakespeare?' The Gipsy Scholar is the quietist *par excellence*, and it may well be that the 'quest' that was to be renewed in the opening stanza of the poem was for this spiritual condition.

Arnold's idea of the soul extends to a belief in survival, and on this subject he has two notions, both sound. The first is that human activity continues.

> In the never-idle work-shop of nature,
> In the eternal movement,

[1] In 1869 he temporarily replaced the last stanza by one containing implications of the by then fashionable theory of evolution: the earlier more visionary presentation is preferable. Arnold was more nearly the complete humanist than Tennyson, and I believe this is the only scientific reference in his poems.

he tells the stricken Brontë sisters,

> Ye shall find yourselves again.

Especially he feels that the strong soul of his father must still be at work.

> In the sounding labour-house vast
> Of being . . .
> Still thou performest the word
> Of the spirit . . .

The other is that man is required to show himself worthy of survival before he can 'mount, and that hardly, to immortal life'. ('Hardly' has been supposed ambiguous, but can only mean 'with difficulty.') This idea of fitness for survival is hinted again in *The Scholar Gipsy*—

> To the just-pausing Genius we remit
> Our worn-out life, and are—what we have been.

If human nature presented itself to Arnold in a generally unattractive light, the natural world upon which man appears to be an interloper was to him an object of almost religious adoration. He voices a feeling akin to the Wordsworthian passion when wishing that he may die gazing out of the window at 'a wide aerial landscape . . . bathed in the sacred dews of morn', gazing till he becomes 'in soul, with what I gaze on, wed . . . the pure, eternal course of life'. We hear a Wordsworthian echo again when he speaks to his heart—

> they
> Which touch thee are unmating things,
> Ocean and clouds and night and day,
> Lorn autumns and triumphant springs.

He longs to escape from the distressful emotions of love to the wind-swept solitudes of the mountains:

> Blow ye winds! lift me with you!
> I come to the wild.
> Fold closely, O Nature!
> Thine arms round thy child.

He says that in his cradle he had been 'breathed on by the rural Pan'. Only once does he speak slightingly of nature: spurred on by 'a preacher's' adoption of the message of Arnold's own sonnet, *Quiet Work*, he declares that

> man hath all that Nature hath, and more,
> And in that *more* lie all his hopes of good.

Of course, he is right in this second sonnet, which expresses an essential truth, while the other is based simply on an analogy, the 'tranquillity' of nature being a quality read into it by the poet, and not anything that man can copy.

Indeed, the weakness of Arnold's treatment of nature is his tendency to anthropomorphism. When, in the poem, *A Wish*, quoted earlier, he says of the natural world that it

> never was the friend of *one*,
> Nor promised love it could not give,
> But lit for all its generous sun,
> And lived itself, and made us live,

he is saying what Wordsworth said in *Tintern Abbey*—

> Knowing that nature never did betray
> The heart that loved her.

But it is plain that Wordsworth meant simply that love for nature will at all times afford consolation against human cares, whereas Arnold, equally plainly, conceives of nature as a living agent, consciously befriending, promising and giving. Wordsworth's personifications of nature do not go beyond the limits of figurative speech, but something more than metaphor is implied in nature's claim, in *The Youth of Nature*, that man can never tell

> Of the thoughts that ferment in my breast,
> My longing, my sadness, my joy.

This is either pantheism or childishness, and there is too much of it. The quite ineffable beauty of the last stanza of *A Summer Night* is a

little flawed by one's sense of the futility of the observation that the
pure dark heavens have no sign of languor, are great and noble,
untroubled and unpassionate. The frequent ascription of 'effortless-
ness' to the workings of nature is similarly dubious. Often the feeling
takes an inoffensive form, as when nature is made to watch the
vicissitudes of humanity 'mild and inscrutably calm'. When Arnold
is imagining on the largest scale he is on safe ground: his cry,

> Murmur of living,
> Stir of existence,
> Soul of the world!

and his invocation of the 'calm soul of all things'—these are lesser
but not less true variants of Wordsworth's

> Wisdom and Spirit of the universe!
> Thou Soul that art the eternity of thought!

Other than in the 'Oxford' poems and a few lyrical passages,
Arnold shows little of Keats's or Tennyson's descriptive powers, nor
of Wordsworth's sensuous contact with nature. We have just a
surface touch of this in his intense pleasure in *coolness*, especially if
associated with greenery or wetness—cool grass, cool rushes, cool
wet turf; also the cool night wind. What he specially does is to take
one of the elements of Wordsworth's genius noted in the *Memorial
Verses*, his 'healing power', and make more conscious use of it than
Wordsworth himself. He finds in nature solace and companionship
and inspiration, and once at least like Wordsworth's Matthew would

> Lie sweetly in the look divine
> Of the slow-sinking sun.

The lesson of *The Scholar Gipsy* and *Thyrsis* is that life with and
according to nature can still constitute an uplifting ideal.

We have already seen that Arnold makes a philosophic error in
contrasting man's mortal life with the apparently unending life of
nature. He argues out at some length, in *The Youth of Nature*, the
question of whether the beauty of nature has an objective reality or

exists only in the mind of the beholder. Coleridge had, in his mood of dejection, declared dismissively,

> we receive but what we give,
> And in our life alone does nature live.

Wordsworth had compromised, suggesting that the imaginative eye half-reveals and half-creates. Arnold asks if it is not the poet's vision that fills us with joy, and allows nature to reply that the greatest poet cannot fully realise the 'loveliness, magic and grace' of the world, nor express even what he does realise. 'The life of the world' is the ultimate reality, and man knows neither it nor himself. Psychology denies this, and is in agreement with Coleridge. Nevertheless, even if Nature lives 'only in our life' it is well for us that she lives. Man is exalted as much by his dreams as by what he sees by daylight.

Before I leave Arnold's nature poetry I would like to draw attention to a fascinating aspect—his treatment of that natural element, water, which covers so much of the earth's surface. Arnold's reaction to water was strange, almost mystic, probably unique. I do not know any other writer who has had—as Arnold, complaining about the pollution of some of the Swiss lakes, told Clough he had—a feeling that water was 'the Mediator between the inanimate and man'. (Yeats carried the idea further—I think too far—in the line, 'What's water but the generated soul?') He will have learnt this feeling from the Lakeland becks, so full of beauty, sparkle, force, purpose, laughter, life; 'Rotha, with thy living wave', he said confidingly. Perhaps he saw another aspect at Laleham—the 'sweet tranquil Thames' of *Philomela*. In one form or another, sea, river or lake, he makes water play a great part in conveying his sense of the character and quality of life, its meaning and its issues.

It is a mistake to suppose that he was obsessed by the river idea, of the 'river of life' carrying man irresistibly forward. Only in *A Dream* do we get this effect, though there forcibly enough:

> the darting river of Life
> (Such now methought it seemed) the river of Life,
> Loud thundering, bore us by; swift, swift it foamed. . . .

But this was in a dream, and it was on second thoughts that Arnold
decided that the swift river of his dream, at first obviously 'a green
Alpine stream', allegorised the way in which circumstances sometimes take control and compel us in directions not in accordance
with our will. In the other river poem, the great and famous poem,
The Future, the river, moving on its destined course, is not life but
time—

> (Man) was born in a ship
> On the breast of the river of Time.

There is no carrying onward: the river, with its varying movements
and surface, the changing world on its banks, is a picturesque
representation of the course of history. The new and vital element
in the picture is provided by the sea, the distant, unknown sea of the
future, ultimately—because described as infinite—the sea of eternity,
whose 'intimations' are figured as 'murmurs and scents'. The river
of life in *A Dream* also carried the occupants of the boat to the sea,
and through landscape reminiscent of that of *The Future*—'burning
plains, bristled with cities'—but there is no hint that this is the sea of
eternity, or anything more than death and extinction. There is a
menacing tone of finality about the last lines:

> Soon the planked cottage by the sun-warmed pines
> Faded—the moss, the rocks; us burning plains,
> Bristled with cities, us the sea received.

Thus in Arnold the sea may stand for death or for eternity, and in
one celebrated instance it is the Sea of Faith, once flowing full but
now ebbing with a grating, melancholy roar. But most often it is
the sea of Life. A river has a direction, and Arnold seldom felt
direction in life—rather 'life's incognisable sea', over which we
'stem by night', or 'life's cold sea' on which he feels the stars shine
not for him. It may stretch to an ocean in *A Summer Night*. A few
men, Arnold tells us, escape from the prison of routine to the 'wide
ocean of life', only to be driven by despotic winds and struck by
tempests as they make for 'some false impossible shore'. In less
destructive but not less sinister wise the sea may be an isolating

quality in life, unplumbed, salt and estranging, that keeps the 'mortal millions'—among them Matthew and Marguerite—apart in spite of 'a longing like despair'. *Resignation* speaks of the 'seas of life and death', both fed from the watershed of a moment.

I cannot agree with the critics who see a figurative reference in every occasion of Arnold's going a-boating—'Still glides the stream, slow drops the boat' . . . but the frequency with which he makes the sea the setting for a poem suggests that it has a more than literal significance for him. There is the 'wide-glimmering sea' in which he and his sister bathed their hands when they came in 'balmy darkness' to the end of their day-long walk. Or the safety of the amber-ceiled, pearl-paved sea to which the forsaken merman and his children retreated before the faithlessness of the beloved mortal. There is certainly something more than salt water about that marvellously realised sea whose waves sucked back the pebbles and then flung them with a grating roar up the beach at Dover. And it is impossible not to feel a sense of the infinite—like that of the sea into which the river of Time was made to flow—in that epic conclusion which shows the mighty Oxus reaching, after a progress now placid now painful,

> His luminous home of waters . . . bright
> And tranquil, from whose floor the new-bathed stars
> Emerge, and shine upon the Aral Sea.

On the other hand, I think it is carrying too far this fact of Arnold's mystical feeling for water to say that it appears in the last stanza of *A Summer Night*—

> Mild o'er her grave, ye mountains, shine!
> Gently by his, ye waters, glide!
> To that in you which is divine
> They were allied.

Why select only the water?—mountains are adduced as well. The lines suggest that Arnold had an even more interesting—because less fanciful—sense of something spiritual, 'divine', in earth itself,

the material globe: a kind of pantheism, though only in a reasonable
degree, not unfelt in Empedocles' invocation of the elements. If it
is not this there would seem to be some confusion of thought.
Normally, to account for the divine spark in man we appeal away
from matter to God. Here Arnold appeals directly to matter, which
is logical only if the implications I have suggested are accepted.
However we interpret this special stanza, nothing can detract from
the beauty and significance of the apotheosis of water which is such
an original and delightful feature of Arnold's nature philosophy.

It may be granted that Arnold, though not to be called a didactic
poet—since his aim is not to teach—is an intellectual poet. He *feels*
his thought, else he were no poet, but his rational mind never ceases
to function, however strongly he may be feeling; the complete
absorption of thought in feeling, resulting in imagination, takes
place only in the very greatest of his poems. This accounts for the
preponderance in his poetry of depreciation of life—a narrowly
rational and unimaginative process. His poetry is largely moral in
spirit, but escapes didacticism because the moral substance is always
passionately conceived, and presented in a poetic style whose grace
seldom falters.

Can we say that such and such is Arnold's philosophy? Of course
not, and there would be something wrong if we could work out a
coherent philosophy from his poetry, which conveys just a number
of strongly felt impressions of life's meaning. These impressions are
embodied rather in single lines or short passages than in whole poems.
Here are some that perhaps represent Arnold more truly than the
preceding sections can claim to do:

> Time . . .
> Brings round to all men
> Some undimmed hours.

> He who flagged not in the earthly strife
> Mounts, and that hardly, to eternal life.

> Ah, Quiet, all things feel thy balm.

Sink, O youth, in thy soul!
Yearn to the greatness of Nature,
Rally the good in the depths of thyself!

The soul. . . .
When it fails, fight as we will, we die;
And while it lasts, we cannot wholly end.

Resolve to be thyself; and know that he
Who finds himself, loses his misery.

he thinks he knows
The hills where his life rose,
And the sea where it goes.

Murmurs and scents of the infinite sea.

In the never idle workshop of nature,
In the eternal movement,
Ye shall find yourselves again.

I don't think any of these has the depth, force and illumination to be found in some from Browning—

Life
Is just our chance of the prize of learning love,

or,

The world's no blot for us,
Nor blank; it means intensely, and means good.

But the lines from Arnold are rich in interest and value, and may be allowed to go some way to redeem the greyness of the earlier picture I felt compelled to draw of the man and his poetry.

CHAPTER II

The Art of Arnold's Poetry

(a)

IT WOULD appear from the preceding chapter that I find the content of Arnold's poetry sometimes false and enervating. Yet I read his poetry with unfading delight. The explanation is, of course, that poetry does *not* 'depend upon the subject', but upon the 'art' that has transformed the subject into poetry. Whether Shakespeare writes cynically about life as a tale told by an idiot or with exaltation about Prospero's vision of the dissolving world, we read with equal pleasure because of the perfect art that has gone to the making of both.

So it is not so important as it might seem that Arnold, from having told Clough in 1848 that the beautiful alone is properly poetical, and in 1849 that form is the sole necessity of poetry, wealth and depth of matter being a superfluity, should in 1853 have settled for the view that poetry (or at least 'modern' poetry) can subsist only by its content. One cannot conceive of great poetry without content, yet how slight, intangible, that content can be. What exquisite aesthetic emotion Rostand charms from a *Petit Chat Noir*, a *Souvenir Vague*, a *Princesse Lointaine!* While Blake opens a window on the infinite with a poem on the tiger burning bright in the forests of the night, de la Mare no less surely opens a smaller one with eight lines on two molluscs gossiping in the light of the rising moon: it is not the animal but the art that counts. Even in the *Preface* that makes so much of content, Arnold admitted that art must be dedicated to joy—the Coleridgean pleasure-principle—which seems to give us all we need. He was over-modest when he told Clough (with the *Empedocles* volume in mind), 'My poems have weight, I think, but no charm.' Weight, perhaps (it depends on your scales), but charm indeed for those who are susceptible to it.

Arnold's 'cool refreshing verse', as Chambers calls it, does more than convey information about subject-matter or the attractive poetic personality behind the verse. Even when poetic passion is but mildly active, the texture of the verse is like that of limpid spring water; the surface shines like a quiet lake under a tranquil sky, as Windermere in *The Prelude*:

> the calm
> And dead-still water lay upon my mind
> Even with a weight of pleasure, and the sky,
> Never before so beautiful, sank down
> Into my heart, and held me like a dream.

Arnold's verse shows feeling under control, emotion singing though bridled. In poetry, both feeling and control must be aesthetic: the poet's emotion must be roused by beauty and those other high essences amid which he is privileged to dwell, and the control must be that of artistic sensibility. In this latter respect Arnold never fails: it is this that makes his irregular verse (not generally a medium to be commended) so completely satisfying. This restraint, the fruit of his classical training, is nothing negative: it is a very positive virtue, but Arnold thought it might be a weakness. He once said he desired a greater 'fullness' in his poetry, but was held back by a 'numbness'. One can agree only to the extent that he seldom, after *The Strayed Reveller*, let himself go, gave himself up to the passion of joy and the beauty of words. He accepted Keats's principle that poetry should be 'great but unobtrusive' rather than his other and perhaps contradictory one that poetry should 'surprise by a fine excess'. His muse was, he said, austere.

'Cool' is Arnold's favourite epithet, water his favourite element, lawn his favourite kind of landscape. This quietness of preference means, among other things, that he can be said to lack the sensuousness of Wordsworth and the colour of Keats. In his approach to

reality through sense-impressions, Wordsworth is unique; but
Arnold has passages where the senses are active:

> Is it then evening
> So soon? I see the night dews,
> Clustered in thick beads, dim
> The agate brooch-stones
> On thy white shoulder;
> The cool night-wind too
> Blows through the portico,
> Stirs thy hair, Goddess,
> Waves thy white robe!

And while no one would claim for him Keats's characteristic
exuberance of colour one has but to turn to *Thyrsis* to find, in the
compass of a few stanzas, blossoms red and white, gold-dusted
snap-dragon, bluebells, white lilies, white and purple fritillaries,
in short, a whole 'high midsummer pomp', with roses, carnations
and daffodils, their colours not mentioned but vividly present to the
mind's eye, and presently an orange and violet sunset. Or the spot
which Iseult chose to tell her children the 'old-world Breton history':

> This cirque of open ground
> Is light and green; the heather, which all round
> Creeps thickly, grows not here, but the pale grass
> Is strewn with rocks, and many a shivered mass
> Of veined white-gleaming quartz, and here and there
> Dotted with holly-trees and juniper.
> In the smooth centre of the opening stood
> Three hollies side by side, and made a screen
> Warm with the winter sun, of burnished green
> With scarlet berries gemmed. . . .

We may note the frequency of white as a colour (like 'cool' as a
sensation)—often used to dilute, as it were, the stronger colours.

All these things are elements in the plain, direct and lucid style
which Arnold acquired through long intimacy with Homer. The
opulence of Shakespeare was alien to him, he ridiculed Swinburne's

'fatal habit of using a hundred words where one would suffice', and delighted to 'esteem Cowper more and more'. His style can sink to the bald, but at its most characteristic it has a beautiful neatness and grace, and sometimes what Saintsbury calls 'a quakerish elegance'.

It was a pity he could not rest content with being entirely competent in his own manner, but must be always criticising the different method of his great contemporary Tennyson. Once he specifically invited comparison, seriously advising Clough to read *Sohrab and Rustum*, which had just been published, side by side with the *Morte d'Arthur*, 'in order to see the difference in *tissue* and *movement* of style'. Though Clough doubtless obeyed instructions there is no record of his reaction, but to me the challenge appears an act of pure madness. For '*tissue*', the verse of *Sohrab and Rustum* is the stuff of a heavy canvas, admirable, lasting, satisfying, taking richly-worked patterns; that of the *Morte* is a marvellously woven silk, equally strong and satisfying, lovely to the touch, exquisitely coloured in grain—a rarer, stranger material, miraculous. And for the second feature, Arnold's verse moves steadily along a noble road over a wide plain under sombre skies, Tennyson's speeds on winged feet through the hills, rising and falling, now swift now slow, with sudden heart-stirring glimpses of unearthly beauty. There was a case for the verse of *Sohrab and Rustum* as against that of some of the *Idylls* (not at that time published), but Arnold's ear (he had no ear for tonal music) should have told him that the *Morte* itself was beyond dispute.

(b)

Let us look more closely at the words Arnold used and the way he used them. Words are the prime material of the poet's art. It is with words, not ideas (as Mallarmé, quoted by Mr Kenneth Allott, said) that poetry is written. There is a sense in which art is synonymous with genius, is certainly the correlative of genius, as inseparable as one side of a coin from the other. In the more practicable sense, art is the way in which the artist uses his materials to the end that he may voice his vision and communicate the imaginative

truth that has come to him through aesthetic experience. The prime
material of the poet's art is words. They are not his only material.
There is also rhythm, not always to be used, but strangely powerful
when its aid is invoked. Words are the prime material of the prose
writer too. His other (optional) material is logic, and Arnold
maintained that prose was more difficult to write than verse
because of the necessity to maintain logical connection. When, in
Parting, the second of the *Switzerland* group of poems, Arnold
keeps moving between his yearning for mountain solitude and
sensations of Marguerite's presence, the connections are anything
but logical, but due to the two lobes of his heart functioning
alternately.

And so, of words, words which some have supposed inadequate
to the thoughts of men and which yet can do what is beyond the
reach of music, of colour and line, of stone or bronze:

> Oh my love, my wife!
> Death that hath sucked the honey of thy breath
> Hath had no power yet upon thy beauty:
> Thou art not conquered; beauty's ensign yet
> Is crimson in thy lips and in thy cheeks,
> And death's pale flag is not advanced there . . .
> . . . never from this palace of dim night
> Will I depart again. . . . Oh here
> Will I set up my everlasting rest,
> And shake the yoke of inauspicious stars
> From this world-wearied flesh.

Glory of words such as this never came Arnold's way, nor indeed
the way of any poet outside the Shakespearean era. But no poet was
ever great without greatness of diction, and Mr Bernard Groom[1]
thinks it was owing to Arnold's failure to attain such greatness of
diction that he failed also to be the greatest poet of his time. It is not
necessary to assent fully to this interesting judgement (which might
be made, with a different qualification, of Browning), but it is true

[1] *The Diction of Poetry from Spenser to Bridges*, by Bernard Groom, University
of Toronto Press, 1955.

that with Arnold language is not itself a thing of supreme greatness, as it is with Shakespeare, Milton and Tennyson. It never has what Gray (quoted by Coleridge) called, 'the pomp and prodigality of heaven'. Nor does he possess that inborn continuous elevation of style—the plateau out of which peaks and dizzy summits can rise effortlessly—which G. M. Hopkins called the 'Parnassien', and which gives *The Excursion* its unbroken sense of nobility. Arnold is unaware of his occasional lapses into banality. Wordsworth's technique was so instinctive that such lapses do not occur: his flatnesses are deliberate and purposeful.

Outside the bare patches Arnold's verbal quality is always satisfying and sometimes inspired. 'Jewels five words long' do not come frequently, and may not dazzle when they do come, but they come easily and leave a sense of delight and admiration. The lover hears Marguerite singing in the distance and exclaims,

> Say, has some wet, bird-haunted English lawn
> Lent it the music of its trees at dawn?

Can there be any who, nursing the fallacy of a disastrous climate, are unable to feel how delicately the word 'wet' images the fresh sweetness of that English morning picture? 'Haunted' is a 'poetical' word, but in the combination used gives a true sense of natural magic. It is partly association that gives the word 'English' its force, but here you have three epithets, of one, of three and of two syllables, with vowels and consonants beautifully varied and ordered —by instinct or fortunate choice—each adding its quota of loveliness to that remembered lawn. The second line is comparatively common-place, but even in the best couplet one verse must be inferior to the other (even in the one about the rose-red city!). Not quite always, though. There is no inequality between the two lines in *The Scholar-Gipsy*—

> Still nursing the unconquerable hope,
> Still clutching the inviolable shade.

Here we have surely that blended music of vowel and consonant which Saintsbury calls 'the glory of English poetry, especially that

D

of the nineteenth century'. How exquisitely the changes are rung between the sounds of 'nursing' and 'clutching', 'unconquerable' and 'inviolable', 'hope' and 'shade'.

It is the excellent choice of words to fit a beautiful and profound sentiment that provides the magical line that closes *The Future*, when man in his ship, floating down the river of time, meets at last, coming upon the night-wind,

> Murmurs and scents of the infinite sea.

Admire again the choice of a dissyllable, a monosyllable and a trisyllable on which to base the dactyls. The same poem affords an example of Arnold's ability to use simpler words with great effectiveness, asking if any poet of today can know God

> With a plainness as near,
> As flashing as Moses felt. . . .

The qualification of 'plainness' by the two words, 'near', signifying intimacy of comprehension, and 'flashing', brilliance of interpretation, illustrates Arnold's faculty of exact expression. And for the effective use of even simpler words we may cite the summation of 'the action of men' at the end of *Empedocles*:

> The day in his hotness,
> The strife with the palm,
> The night in her silence,
> The stars in their calm.

(Note the succession of pronouns.) Or the much but not too-much anthologised *Requiescat*, which will bear comparison with the last of the *Lucy* poems. Both poems are written in the plainest language, though Wordsworth's one unusual word, *diurnal*, adds much to the effect, as do the repetitions in Arnold's first three stanzas, and the beautifully chosen words in 'Her cabin'd, ample spirit'.

What intense evocation of sight is produced by the words telling how the majestic river Oxus flowed on under the solitary moon, 'brimming, and bright, and large', and of sound in the 'melancholy, long, withdrawing roar' (Arnold would have shuddered at Mr Jump's suggestion that there was an intended 'near-rhyme' in 'draw' and 'roar') of the waves on Dover beach. The classical instinct for rightness is behind the choice of words, but the right words spring from the poet's own individual vision, and so present their objects in a new light, as poetry must or be vain. The word *moon-blanched* is such an individual word. Arnold discovered it in 1852, for the poem *A Summer Night*—'In the deserted moon-blanched street'. In the following year, printing *The Scholar-Gipsy*, he used the word again, the white sheep being seen to cross 'the strips of moon-blanched green' (evocation of sight again extra-ordinarily vivid). And in 1867 we find the sea meeting the 'moon-blanched sand' in *Dover Beach*. The three-fold repetition is technically a fault (and only the requirements of metre prevent the word *moon* being expressed instead of understood in *The Forsaken Merman*, where 'high rocks throw mildly on the blanched sands a gloom'), but we can forgive it since the word gives fresh pleasure each time we meet it in a new context.

Mr F. W. Bateson calls in question some of Arnold's adjectives as unnecessary. 'Ah! pale ghosts, rejoice!'—aren't ghosts always pale? Mr Bateson asks. But Coleridge has 'the white foam flew', Milton 'the ethereal sky', and half the adjectives in the *Elegy* are 'unnecessary' if one probes them with a pin instead of rejoicing in their beauty of effect.

Mr Eliot says (as he must if he is not to condemn half the poetry of his period) that the words used in poetry need not always be beautiful. Few words are beautiful in themselves, but most words may become beautiful in combination, just as 'touch' in piano-playing cannot be realised in a single note but only in a succession. Poetry may be defined as a transformation of words under poetic feeling, and the sense of words is the sense of poetry. Arnold's sense of words was discontinuous, and his first versions (as shown in the critical apparatus provided by Tinker and Lowry) are sometimes painfully gauche. His revisions were generally admirable, but Mr Groom points out that he did not always take trouble to remedy poor work. The sonnet *Religious Isolation* is simply bad, and the last stanza of *Self-Deception* little better. Two small defects that cause me disproportionate annoyance are to be found in those all-but-perfect poems *The Scholar-Gipsy* and *Thyrsis*. In the former, one stanza describes the Gipsy as

> Rapt, twirling in thy hands a withered spray,

the next as

> Wrapt in thy cloak and battling with the snow.

In successive stanzas of *Thyrsis* 'the tree' is referred to as 'the signal elm' and 'that single elm-tree'.[1] It is quite true, as has been pointed out, that *ask'st*, in the *Sonnet to a Friend*, is unpronounceable, but there is no reason why one should not say *askest*: no one supposes that elision demands complete removal of the syllable, or that when Milton wrote *th'arch-angel* he intended us to say *tharch-angel*. But why Arnold did not make the line unobjectionable by putting 'you ask' I cannot imagine. He has some poor rhymes—*dawning* and *morning*, *fire* and *by her*—and an occasional untidy stanza, like this from *Obermann II*—

> Some secrets may the poet tell,
> For the world loves new ways;
> To tell too deep ones is not well—
> It knows not what he says,

and two stanzas in the *Grande Chartreuse* beginning, 'Ah, if it *be* passed, take away . . .' Tennyson would not have allowed these. It is amusing to note that Arnold (who was deaf to Tennyson's perfection of form) altered the line in *Sohrab and Rustum*,

> And if indeed the one desire rules all

---

[1] One hates noticing such flaws in a work of art, because once seen they are always there. That lovely poem, Stevenson's *Requiem*, has been spoilt for me by my continual awareness of the repetition of the word *grave*, as noun and verb, within its exiguous compass.

to

> And if the one desire indeed rules all,

because Clough suggested that the first version had a Tennysonian
movement.

But when we deprecate the lack of critical care that permitted
these small lapses, we must set beside them such wonderful improve-
ments as were made, for instance, in *Philomela*, where the unforget-
table epithet for the nightingale, 'tawny-throated', was first written
inken-throated (see also p. 122 for this), and the whole of the second
stanza was (as again Tinker and Lowry show) originally composed in
an incredibly inferior form. Of the 'inadequacies and incompetences
of expression' that Saintsbury saw in *The Forsaken Merman* I myself
cannot find a single one: he did not specify.

The most famous, and most widely accepted (if least interesting)
definition of poetry is Coleridge's 'the best words in the best order'.
That 'best order' may or may not result in rhythmic form, but when
it does the poet is provided with a tool of enormous power. Rhythmic form is more than metre, and more than simple rhythm, which
may occur in prose—though even of rhythm Goethe said there was
something magical in it: 'it makes us believe that the sublime lies
within our reach'. Rhythmic form arises when rhythm seizes on
metre and moulds it to an effect like that of music, transporting
the reader, body and soul, into a state in which he feels he is more
closely in contact with the poet's mind, and perhaps with reality
itself, than he could become by any other means. It is one form of
Eliot's 'auditory imagination', penetrating far below the conscious
levels of thought and feeling. (An even later school of criticism
calls it *dope*.) Of the three companion poets, Tennyson, Browning
and Arnold, Tennyson is a master of this effect, Browning rarely
attains it. With Arnold the poetic impulse is not often born deep
enough for rhythmic form to result, but he was obviously stirred
profoundly by the romance and passion of the Tristram story, and
it seems to me that there breaks through, here and there in Parts I
and II of *Tristram and Iseult*, a movement that conveys something

more, something more significant, than words alone could. The beautiful flow, in conception and execution, of *The Forsaken Merman*, has a music of its own, not, I think, rising to rhythmic form, but the poems in genuine irregular metre, notably *Dover Beach* and *The Future*, include this element in the perfect art of their composition, so that waves of rhythm lift the spirit into close communion with the poet's imagination. This is unexpected, because irregular form does not often lend itself to the effect under notice, but the kind was congenial to Arnold. I find the rhythmic pulse beating once more in *A Dream*: it rises slowly through the blank verse of that poignantly conceived poem, gathering force till it breaks in a rushing lifting wave in the last eight lines. Generally, metres of less than five feet do not lend themselves to rhythmic form, but sometimes short unrhymed measures, under Arnold's mastery, may catch up the true poetic impulse and inspiration and communicate them to the reader, so that we are able to experience all the suggestive force of a passage like this:

> Loveliness, magic and grace,
> They are here! they are set in the world.
> They abide; and the finest of souls
> Hath not been thrilled by them all,
> Nor the dullest been dead to them quite.
> The poet who sings them may die,
> But they are immortal and live,
> For they are the life of the world.
> Will ye not learn it, and know,
> When ye mourn that a poet is dead,
> That the singer was less than his themes,
> Life, and emotion, and I?

A result of the classical clarity of Arnold's style is that—more than with any other nineteenth-century poet—everything he has to say is said with perfect intelligibility: with one exception—*The New Sirens*. This poem conveys nothing at all to me. Arnold had to supply a 'commentary' for Clough's benefit, but the commentary is no more understandable than the poem, and seems to bear little relation to it.

(c)

The normal poetic skills Arnold has in abundance. As a rule he handles his numerous metres and stanza forms expertly. He does not invent much, and the one instance of his attempting an original stanza form (the *Thyrsis* stanza is a brilliant expansion from Keats) was not successful. In *Empedocles* he makes the philosopher express his views to Pausanias in a stanza of four short lines, rhyming *a b a b*, followed by a longer one apparently unrhymed but really rhyming with the corresponding long line in the next stanza. The separation of the two rhyming hexameters is too wide, and the effect of rhyme is lost, while the awkwardness of the one line apparently hanging loose in the first stanza of each pair fidgets like a lump in a mattress. How much more successful Browning was with the more inventive stanza of *Rabbi Ben Ezra*. But the variegated simple stanzas, mostly in short lines, of *Switzerland*; the involved stanza of *Thyrsis* and *The Scholar-Gipsy*; the playful dactyls of *Separation* and the meditative trochees of *The New Sirens*—all these, and others, to suit differing moods and purposes, are managed with accomplished ease. And everywhere are the classical smoothness and restraint; the civilised measures do not excite but tranquillise; the ornate is simply absent; everything is exquisitely patterned and beautifully right, as in an ordered garden.

Rhyme does not generally inspire Arnold, and perhaps sometimes hinders. The penultimate and antepenultimate stanzas of *A Southern Night* owe their infelicitousness to the difficulty Arnold found in expressing his thought in the necessary rhymed stanza formation:

> And what but gentleness untired,
>   And what but noble feeling warm,
> Wherever shown, howe'er inspired,
>   Is grace, is charm?

> What else is all these waters are,
>   What else is steeped in lucid sheen,
> What else is bright, what else is fair,
>   What else serene?

Yet neither was blank verse a native function with Arnold, and in its use he stands inferior to the other romantics, indeed to all the major poets. His best piece in this kind is the short poem, *A Dream*, where the blank verse is of a genuine spoken order, alive and flexible, as good as Tennyson's in *Dora*, or Browning at his best. His longest, *Balder Dead*, goes (appropriately enough) at a leaden pace, and reads like an extremely competent translation: it may have been intended for schools, as an introduction to the grand Norse epics. But the verse of *Sohrab and Rustum* is quite magnificent, though with too little variation till the concluding paragraph is reached. This famous passage owes its magic chiefly to the choice of words—including proper names effectively spaced—suiting the mood of serenity that follows the pain and conflict of the tale; but the verse too moves with a sinuous grace that furthers the desired impression of tranquil progress to a satisfying end. Saintsbury called it Tennysonian; I hear more of Milton in it, but feel it has so much of individual quality that other poets may be forgotten. The blank verse that concludes *Mycerinus* (after the rather dull sextains that precede) moves more swiftly, but that of *Empedocles* has little to be said for it: it is roughened and slightly colloquialised for the purpose of drama, but the colloquialism is not integrated with the verse, as always in Browning. But there is some excellent blank verse to be dug out of *Merope* (e.g. in Aepytus's account of the hunt and the drowning of 'stag, dogs and hunter') by those who have patience to go through that somewhat tedious but not altogether unrewarding imitation of a Sophoclean tragedy.

Of greater interest is the shortened blank verse that Arnold used for some of his elegiac poems and some others.[1] It is seen at its best in *Rugby Chapel*, where each line consists (with very slight variation) of a dactyl or a trochee followed (always) by a dactyl and a single stressed syllable:

> Ó strŏng| sóul, bў whăt| shóre
> Tárrĭest thŏu| nów? Fŏr thăt| fórce . . .

[1] Mr Kingsmill dismisses all Arnold's shorter measures as 'doggerel'.

Heine's Grave and *Haworth Churchyard* also are written, with less distinction, in this metre. It might easily have become monotonous, but does not, though it could not go on for long because of the small number of possible variations, confined as these are to the first foot. The metre is employed in *The Youth of Nature* and *The Youth of Man*, with an occasional shorter or longer line. Oddly attractive is the even shorter measure adopted for *Consolation*—lines consisting of a dactyl and a trochee (sometimes another dactyl or a single syllable) grouped in fives:

> Mist clogs the|sunshine
> Smoky dwarf houses
> Hem me round everywhere
> A vague dejection
> Weighs down my soul.

Arnold (like Browning) makes much use of trochaic measures. Part I of *Tristram and Iseult*, called *Tristram*, is in iambic; at the end of this part a fine swift couplet in anapaests switches us over to the trochaic form in which Part II, *Iseult of Ireland*, is cast:

> What voices are these on the clear night-air?
> What lights in the court—what steps on the stair?
>
> Raise the light, my page, that I may see her.—
>   Thou hast come at last then, haughty Queen!
> Long I've waited, long I've fought my fever;
>   Late thou comest, cruel thou hast been.

Part III, *Iseult of Brittany*, reverts to iambic.

There are two groups of sonnets, one in the first, 1849, volume, and the other in the last, 1867. All are in the Petrarchan form, with the Wordsworthian variation in lines 6 and 7 (Arnold was never willing to hunt for rhymes), and most are written in strict compliance with the requirements of sonnet form. The later sonnets do not differ from the earlier ones, except that they are more Miltonic in tone. Each group has at least one very fine sonnet. The early one on Shakespeare is acknowledged to be among the supreme sonnets of the language. The later one, *Austerity of Poetry*, treats its significant subject nobly, but exhibits a flaw or two: 'tried to blow' is a feeble expression, and the triple repetition of *bride*, together with the two internal rhyme-words, *tried* and *outside*, is an example of Arnold's lack of technical care. But I want to stress again that such carelessness is rare. Over the great majority of his poetry we can enjoy the varied music of metre and syllable, consonant and vowel, blended into verse and stanza with complete mastery. Though he makes sparse use of rhythmic form his best things, says Saintsbury, bring about the true poetic intoxication.

Arnold experimented with 'free verse' as no other nineteenth-century poet did. Before him there had been only the choruses of *Samson Agonistes*, for which Milton adopted 'free verse' to parallel the lyric chorus of the Greek plays. (Wordsworth's *Ode* is so firmly bound by its rhymes that it can hardly be called 'free'.) The verse of *The Strayed Reveller* is more 'free' than that of any other poem outside the twentieth century, being nothing but prose broken up into short irregular lines, yet it achieves a rare beauty. That of *Dover Beach* and *The Future* is strangely effective in producing poetic transport. All these poems will come under full examination in a later chapter. They seem to disprove Mr Eliot's assertion that only a bad poet would welcome 'free verse' as a liberation from form.

The words 'classic' and 'romantic' hover round Arnold's head. His style is accepted as classical; for the substance and spirit of his poetry he is condemned by Mr James as a 'declined romantic'. This we shall look into presently, but on the whole it is obvious that Arnold's aim at a serene simplicity of diction, a balanced and well-proportioned style, is a classical one. Even when torn between Marguerite's charms and his passionate desire to get away from her to the mountain solitudes he keeps the hand of restraint on the verse. He shares the classical ideals of law and order in language, and does not indulge the individualism of the romantic. But his style is personal enough to be at its best recognisable in quotation. His diction is civilised but not dead (Raleigh suggested that a classic was a dead romantic). His style is most clearly seen to be classical in contrast to the description of the other kind given by C. H. Herford: 'Style is Romantic in proportion as it presents its object not simply and directly but through a glamour of imagery and emotion which, according to the quality of the poet, obscures or reveals.'

One of the items in Arnold's classical habit is that he did not go out of his way to invent words—as Browning so often and sometimes so painfully did. Arnold's only species of innovation (pointed out by Mr Groom and M. Bonnerot) results from his fondness for negative words in *un-*. Some of his best known phrases include words thus prefixed: *the unplumbed, salt, estranging sea*; *unwavering deep disdain*; *the unwrinkled Rhine*; *the unregarded river of our life*; and (one that Wordsworth might have envied) *uncrumpling fern*. The *Laocoon* poem has *safe unwandering feet*, *unpausing* and *unrelaxing*, *Self-Dependence* has, within a few lines, *unaffrighted, undistracted, unregardful*. *A Summer Night* begins with silent white windows *unopening down*, goes on to *the old unquiet breast*, and includes in its course *unmeaning, unfreed, unblest, undebarred, untroubled, unpassionate*. The nineteenth stanza of *Thyrsis* has two beautiful expressions in *the west unflushes* and *the morningless and unawakening sleep*, and *Empedocles* has in two lines *the unallied unopening earth* and *the unrecognising sea*. And there is that bitter epigram which describes man as *an aimless unallayed desire*. Possibly a weakness, but an unconscious and endearing one.

(d)

Arnold did not, like Shakespeare and Browning, think in metaphor, except for his continuous preoccupation with life as a sea or a river, which has been illustrated. Otherwise his metaphors are few and simple. He will warn Marguerite that

> A sea rolls between us,
> Our different past;

Iseult of Brittany is always for him a flower, a snowdrop; the vale of earth is overshadowed by the mountains of necessity; the furnace of the world shrivels man's spirit. He constantly personifies Nature:

the Pillar broods and Egremont sleeps and Rotha is invoked to
keep fresh the grass on Wordsworth's grave. But there are no great
metaphors, pregnant and illuminating, like

> Life's but a walking shadow, a poor player
> That frets and struts his hour,

or,

> Greek endings, each the little passing-bell
> That signifies some faith's about to die.

When Arnold really intends to call metaphor to his aid he does it
deliberately and with complete success. *The Future* begins,

> A wanderer is man from his birth.
> He was born in a ship
> On the breast of the River of Time.

At first it looks as if it is the life of individual man that is to be
represented as a voyage (as the River of Life bore the Dreamer away
from Marguerite), but presently we see humanity sailing down the
ages to reach the unknown sea of the future, or of eternity. The
metaphor is carried through the poem (which thus doubtless becomes
an allegory) and elaborated in some of the most glorious poetry
Arnold ever wrote. So too he works out in the liveliest detail his
vision of lonely human 'islands' separated by the estranging sea, but
linked at times by the song of nightingales, when

> lovely notes from shore to shore
> Across the sands and channels pour.

More briefly, but with equal vividness and care for detail, he
describes in *Dover Beach* the 'sea of Faith', once at the full but now
ebbing drearily. In *Palladium* the image of the soul as a high-built
temple is supremely handled.

It is the same with the simile. We are here 'as on a darkling plain';
the Tartar tents 'cluster like beehives'. More imaginatively, the
soul is like a windborne spinning mirror catching the light in
glimpses; the beauty and grace of nature are hard to discern,

> Like stars in the deep of the sky
> Which arise on the glass of the sage
> But are lost when their watcher is gone.

A string of Shelleyan similes begins *The Voice*—

> As the kindling glances,
> Queen-like and clear,
> Which the bright moon lances
> From her tranquil sphere . . .

As arising in the course of composition, Arnold's similes are few and commonplace: how fresh and original beside them is the plainest of Browning's—the bough

> white with coming buds
> Like the bright side of a sorrow,

or the trees bending over the forest-pool 'as wild men watch a sleeping girl'. But, having written the whole of *The Scholar-Gipsy*, up to the last two stanzas, without a sign of a simile (unless perhaps in the reference to Dido), Arnold devotes those last two stanzas, or nineteen lines of them, to the famous simile about the Tyrian trader. And it is the considered effort of the extended simile that is Arnold's speciality, one that he shares with Milton and Browning; these three take the comparatively simple extended simile of Homer and make of it a figure of surpassing interest. The two narrative poems exemplify the habit. *Sohrab and Rustum* contains seven extended similes (one as long as the *Gipsy* tail-piece) and a number of half-extended ones. They hold up the stately course of the narrative, but pleasantly enough: they grow with easy naturalness out of the verse and always have a beauty and interest of their own, like the brilliant one which tells that the royal sign on Sohrab's arm was

> in faint vermilion points
> Prick'd, as a cunning workman, in Pekin,
> Pricks with vermilion some clear porcelain vase,
> An emperor's gift—at early morn he paints,
> And all day long, and, when night comes, the lamp
> Lights up his studious forehead and his hands.

And there are about as many in the course of *Balder Dead*: a particularly vivid one ends the tale—

> And as a stork which idle boys have trapped,
> And tied him in a yard, at autumn sees
> Flocks of his kind pass flying o'er his head
> To warmer lands and coasts that keep the sun;—
> He strains to join their flight, and from his shed
> Follows them with a long complaining cry—
> So Hermod gazed, and yearned to join his kin.

I have noticed only one simile in *Alaric*, but *Cromwell* is sown thickly with similes of a plain manufactured kind:

> And peaceful joys and gentler thoughts swept by,
> Like summer lightnings o'er a darkened sky;
> The peace of childhood and the thoughts that roam
> Like loving shadows round that childhood's home.

Onomatopeia, which Tennyson handles so brilliantly, seems to be absent, and alliteration, Browning's pet device, is inconspicuous.

Alaric at Rome must be the dullest poem ever written by a budding major poet. Wordsworth's *Evening Walk* (written at the same age) is attractive in comparison. The *Cromwell* displays much more power. The comparison here is with *Pauline*—both poems belong to their authors' twenty-first year. There is, as a matter of fact, no comparison, Browning's poem showing throughout qualities of greatness and genius quite absent from Arnold's. But, given the occasion, an uncongenial set subject in a set form, the result is not to be despised. The Popian couplets are pumped out by regular piston-beats, with plenty of bi-valve lines—

> The shout of onset and the shriek of fear
> Smote, like the rush of waters, on his ear;
> And his eye kindled with the kindling fray,
> The surging battle and the mailed array!

There are echoes of *Childe Harold*, of Gray's *Bard* and *The Progress of Poesy*, of the *Morte d'Arthur*. And there are some excellent passages, such as that (55-64) describing the growth in Cromwell's youth of 'an inward light', and that (140-158) narrating his 'long vision of the years to be'. The decasyllabic couplet was not used again except— and there to very different effect—in parts of *Tristram and Iseult*, whose brilliant variety of form will be looked at later. The two long blank verse narratives have received enough attention for the present.

I mention the touching 'later poem', *Geist's Grave*, only because Middleton Murry thought it the best thing of its kind ever written —he cannot have read the *Last Words to a Dumb Friend*, where Hardy's genius for regret leaves Arnold's pathos far behind.

(e)

Quotable lines arise when striking thought is expressed with finished art or fine craftsmanship. That perfection of style is more important than profundity of thought is shown by the superiority in this respect of Pope and Tennyson over Dryden and Browning. Arnold's thought is often sound and original, but brilliance of expression does not always come to hand at the required moment— except in those two poems where art and imagination achieve complete fusion, *Thyrsis* and *The Scholar-Gipsy*. Outside these two, which will be considered in their place, I find but few quotable lines and couplets.

Some have already been noticed, like the lovely distich describing Marguerite's voice—

> Say, has some wet, bird-haunted English lawn
> Lent it the music of its trees at dawn?—

or her eyes—

> Eyes too expressive to be blue,
> Too lovely to be grey,

and Urania's with their

> Pure, unwavering deep disdain.

There is the great line,

>   The unplumbed, salt, estranging sea,

and this of the night-sky,

>   Plainness and clearness without shadow of stain.

Of poets we have

>   Wordsworth's healing power,

of Shakespeare,

>   Others abide our question, thou art free,

and of Sophocles,

>   Who saw life steadily and saw it whole.

A useful brevity on life (applicable also to art)—

>   But tasks in hours of insight willed
>   Can be through hours of gloom fulfilled.

This one of Merlin and Vivien attracts by sheer beauty of sound—

>   For she was passing weary of his love

(which, however, was borrowed out of Malory).

There are longer passages, some of which can stand with almost anything that can be quoted from the poets.

From *Dover Beach*:

>   The Sea of Faith
>   Was once too at the full, and round earth's shore
>   Lay like the folds of a bright girdle furled.
>   But now I only hear
>   Its melancholy, long, withdrawing roar,
>   Retreating, to the breath
>   Of the night-wind, down the vast edges drear
>   And naked shingles of the world.

From *The Future*:

> And the width of the waters, the hush
> Of the grey expanse where he floats,
> Freshening its current and spotted with foam
> As it draws to the Ocean, may strike
> Peace to the soul of the man on its breast—
> As the pale waste widens around him,
> As the banks fade dimmer away,
> As the stars come out, and the night-wind
> Brings up the stream
> Murmurs and scents of the infinite sea.

From *Tristram's* dream:

> All red with blood the whirling river flows,
> The wide plain rings, the dazed air throbs with blows.
> Upon us are the chivalry of Rome—
> Their spears are down, their steeds are bathed in foam.
> 'Up, Tristram, up,' men cry, 'thou moonstruck knight!
> What foul fiend rides thee? On into the fight!'
> —Above the din her voice is in my ears;
> I see her form glide through the crossing spears—
> Iseult! . . . .

There is the marvellous close of *Sohrab and Rustum*; there are the lines in *A Summer Night* about the pale master driving through the tempest for some false impossible shore, and ten lines about the poet's mighty heart from *Resignation*, and the two stanzas of *Obermann II* about the patient East bowing before the legions, and almost any stanza from *The Scholar-Gipsy* or *Thyrsis*. Not all of these are in the top class, but most of them are, and they have the recognisable thrilling touch that bespeaks the great poet.

(f)

A word must be said about the ambiguous position of Keats in Arnold's poetry and criticism. Up to 1853 he could hardly speak too

E

angrily of Keats, his diction, his character and his influence. In the essay written for Ward's *Poets* in 1880 he speaks with no less passion of the 'fascinating felicity' and 'perfection of loveliness' in Keats's poetic expression, of the 'flint and iron' in his character, and of his place with Shakespeare. But this reversal is only to say that he had by this time read Keats with the necessary intensity, and that his critical powers had matured. And even while he was finding nothing but faults in Keats, he was absorbing something of his form and spirit, though less than Mr Ford[1] supposes. I cannot think that because Keats mentions 'the fume of poppies' in the *Ode to Autumn* we are to believe that Arnold's line in *The Scholar-Gipsy*, 'Through the thick corn the scarlet poppies peep', was not the result of his own observation; and it is equally unlikely that the word *borne* in 'The bleating of the folded flocks is borne' was suggested by its homophone in 'Full-grown lambs loud-bleat from hilly bourne'. It seems unnecessary to suppose that the series of personifications of Autumn as a thresher, a reaper, a gleaner and a cider-presser gave Arnold even a 'hint' for the search for the elusive Gipsy; just as the immortality Arnold imagined for his wandering mystic is entirely different from, and therefore not likely to have been suggested by, the immortality predicated by Keats of his nightingale.

Nevertheless, it is clear that from the beginning the genius of Keats imposed itself on Arnold's mind, for Arnold was not a violently original poet like Wordsworth or Browning. The spirit of *Endymion* informs *The Strayed Reveller*, and the diction of the early Keats is traceable in some of Callicles' songs. But the Keatsian influence is most marked, as Mr Ford shows, in the descriptive parts of *Tristram and Iseult*, although in that poem the feelings and words of the lovers are individualised into a high passion that stems partly from mediaeval romance and partly from that by no means un-admirable thing, mid-nineteenth-century sentiment: it certainly owes little to Keats, so mature in genius but emotionally so youthful.

Let us revert to Mr Groom and his suggestion that deficiency in style kept Arnold from achieving an outstanding position—indeed

[1] *Keats and the Victorians*, by G. H. Ford, Yale, 1944.

the highest—among Victorian poets. Mr Groom is specifically referring to Arnold's diction, but—extending his formula to embrace the whole term, art—I am constrained to ask, can art be incommensurate with genius? The answer is plain. There is no single example of a great poet, from Chaucer to de la Mare, whose art—diction, form, imagery—is not an integral and equal part of his genius. It must be so. A mortal who has been gifted by the gods with a new vision of truth and beauty will have been granted also the power to communicate his vision. A mute Milton is a contradiction. And Arnold's poetic genius being great but limited, high but not overtowering, so his lovely and adorable art achieves but rarely that supremacy which belongs to the supreme poet. We may remember his own estimate—unnecessarily modest—'My poems, viewed absolutely, are certainly little or nothing'. The word 'absolutely' introduces considerations that must be held over for my last chapter.

CHAPTER III

The Love-poems

A RNOLD'S love-poetry is possibly the least important part of his writing: it is certainly the least regarded. 'Marguerite', the 'dark lady' of the poems, has received an almost embarrassing amount of attention, but the poems themselves have not been thought worthy of critical study. For myself, his love-poetry was what first attracted me to Arnold, perhaps because it was so different from Browning's, to me the ideal. It has a personal intimacy hardly found elsewhere; it is informed by an astringent emotion that touches the heart more poignantly than the sultrier passions of the greater love-poets. It is everywhere unhappy, like the complicated loves of the *Sonnets*, and indulges a brooding meditativeness only paralleled in Donne. And—partly, I suppose, because of the injunction on a biography—an atmosphere of mystery attaches to the situation. We do not know who was the object of the poems, what were Arnold's relations with her, or indeed if she existed at all. And yet this is genuine love-poetry.

There are less than twenty 'love-poems' (some critics would take in a few poems which would bring the total to just over twenty), and they were all written between Arnold's twenty-sixth and thirtieth years. There is no record, poetical or otherwise, of his having followed 'a young man's fancy', but, experiencing love rather late, he proceeded to get love-poetry (if not love) out of his system. Most of the poems were printed in the early volumes (1849 and 1852), without linkage or classification, but later Arnold arranged twelve of them in two groups called *Switzerland* and *Faded Leaves*. The *Switzerland* group of seven poems, together with two other poems called *A Memory Picture* and *A Dream*, statedly concern themselves with a girl or woman called Marguerite. No name is given to the subject of the other group, and Mr Kenneth Allott writes[1] that it is now generally accepted that the *Switzerland* poems were inspired by a French girl, Marguerite, whom Arnold met on holiday in Thun in 1848 and 1849, and that *Faded Leaves* was inspired by Frances Lucy Wightman, whom he met in 1849 and married in 1851.

I am not aware of sufficient grounds for such general acceptance. Little is known in detail about this period of Arnold's life. All that we have is contained in, or can be deduced from, the letters to Clough, and only two of the letters have any bearing on the love story. On September 29, 1848, Arnold, writing from the Baths of Leuk, said, 'Tomorrow I . . . get to Thun, linger one day at the Hotel Bellevue for the sake of the blue eyes of one of its inmates, and then proceed. . . .' It is natural to suppose that these are the blue-grey eyes of Marguerite, and most readers feel justified in ignoring Arnold's declaration to his daughters that she was a figment of his imagination: Chambers is pleasantly ironic about this.

But later in the same letter there is a passage which seems to me likely to be connected with the affair in progress, and which certainly throws a new light on Arnold. He speaks of Béranger, whom he has been reading on his travels, and says he has got tired of him, adding the odd comment that he is glad to be tired of a writer—there is so much to be known and explored that it is well to get one tract of it tucked away and done with. And he continues, 'More particularly is this my feeling with regard to (I hate the word) women. We know beforehand all they can teach us, yet we are obliged to learn it directly from them.' This is, I suppose, the only link between Arnold and Kipling, whose philosopher-soldier, you remember, had taken his fun where he found it, had had his picking of sweethearts, and after each experience was able to say, 'An' I learned about women from 'er'. I think it is clear that Arnold, though he was going back for another day with Marguerite's blue eyes,

[1] Article in *The Times Literary Supplement*, March 1958.

believed he had 'tired' of her, and that the chapter was now closed, leaving him with new-old knowledge of—though he hated the generalised word—women.

He goes on, after this piece of self-revelation, to write, for Clough's benefit, ten lines of excellent but quite uncharacteristic blank verse, to the effect that since a woman is lovely for a moment only, that moment may be less important than the long 'before', when she did not exist, and the long 'after' when she will be 'most unlovely'. Arnold is often bitter, but I do not know any place in his published poetry where he is as cynical as this, though the gist of the thought, put less brutally, is in the last stanza of *Horatian Echo*, written a year earlier. In any case, things were not as completely over and finished as he supposed, and almost exactly a year later he writes from Thun, 'I am here in a curious and not altogether comfortable state', and proceeds to copy out a stanza from the poem *Parting*, published three years later and afterwards made the second poem in the *Switzerland* group.

All this is more colourful than factual, and, the information being so obligingly scanty, I propose to treat the two main groups just as 'love-poems', with a common subject, 'Marguerite'. The dazzling Academy portrait—as by Sargent or Frank Salisbury—of Marguerite in *Switzerland* is not appreciably varied in *Faded Leaves*, and the meeting 'too late' bewailed in one of the poems in the second group does not seem applicable to the circumstances of Arnold's acquaintance with Miss Wightman. The feeling of the two groups is continuous, and as the poems were printed together in 1852 and only later arranged in the two named groups I think it permissible to regard the portrait as a composite if not a single one, with the name Marguerite firmly attached.

It has been suggested that Marguerite is 'a symbol of Arnold's youthful self'. This is both unconvincing and dull. It is less improbable that she was an idealised memory, Shelley's *amans amare*, Browning's *Pauline*. Can we suppose that Wordsworth, on one of his walks with the young Arnold, confided to him the story of Annette, thus placing in the boy's mind (remember he copied the elder poet to the extent of italicising words in poetry) the idea that he too might one day have an adventure (a less desperate one, though Wordsworth would only have given him the romantic outline) with a French girl before settling down to an English marriage? Of course we can suppose nothing of the sort. All we can say is that something of actual, something of dream, went to the creation of the real yet shadowy picture built up in Arnold's imagination from his teasing impressions of the blue-eyed girl of Thun. She set a bell chiming in his heart, and, at intervals from 1849 to 1857, the echoes issued in poems—one in 1849, a whole flock in 1852, others in 1853, 1855 and 1857, and a belated one, tender and true yet somewhat harsh and jangled, in 1867.

I have called Marguerite a shadow because Arnold's relations with her were probably tentative and brief, and the poems but the emanations of memory; yet for a shadow her personality is singularly distinct—more so than other poets have made their more substantial loves. And a very attractive personality it is, as befits the beloved of the poet who versified her. Marguerite's poet was the gay Disraelian dandy not long down from Oxford, where he had been described by Principal Shairp as blithe and debonair, sparkling with banter when not half a-dream with poetry, and by Max Müller as a figure 'beautiful and Olympian, Jove-like'. This young man was not likely, at twenty-six, to 'fall for' anything far short of perfection, and if the young woman presented to us with this degree of realism has her share of faults, these are only such as to make her, as they say, more desirable.

Let me first dispose of a silly cavil that was raised at the time and was still current fifty years later. The first of the Marguerite poems, the only one which, to judge by date of publication (1849), was written 'on the spot', as it were, had for its refrain,

> Ere the parting kiss be dry,
> Quick, thy tablets, Memory!

This harmless hyperbole furnished an additional weapon for those 'friends' who had already 'ridiculed a tender leave-taking', and gave rise to references to 'Marguerite of the wet kisses'. One wonders if these nice objectors had ever done more than plant a chaste peck on the cheek of a not-too-favourite aunt. The invidious expression means simply that Marguerite not only accepted but returned Matthew's kiss, but the sensitive poet was sufficiently put out by the jibes to replace hyperbole by tautology—

> Ere the parting hour go by,
> Quick, thy tablets, Memory!

The poem lost an element of actuality, but remains delightful.

Marguerite, it seems, was a pretty girl, perhaps even a lovely woman. A 'daughter of France', she yet had 'sweet blue eyes', though there are suggestions that they may have been grey, and the doubt gave rise to the exquisite lines,

> Eyes too expressive to be blue,
> Too lovely to be grey.

Just so her hair is now brown, now 'ash-coloured', but is always soft and once 'enkerchiefed'. (The logic that would infer from this that she was a house-maid is a little strained.) Her cheek is pale, her voice is sweet, her figure is graceful. Of course.

These are of the lover's staple. But Arnold discovered a trait in Marguerite that had not previously been celebrated in a mistress. This was archness, that conscious but innocent exercise of charm which is pleasing or sickening according to the quality of the woman exercising it and the feeling towards her of the man for whose benefit it is being exercised. I cannot find that any other poet employs the word when erotically occupied. Tennyson calls the baby Lilian 'innocent-arch', and Wordsworth confines his usages of the term to a child of three, a parrot and a satirically observed 'model' scholar.[1] But Arnold found the attribute, as exhibited by Marguerite, irresistible, and he does not stop at what some might call damnable iteration. In the *Memory Picture* she has 'the archest

---

[1] Arnold said of *Tam Glen* that it represented Burns 'at his archest and soundest', a somewhat puzzling judgement which does not throw much light on Marguerite.

chin mockery ever ambushed in', in *Switzerland* it is her smile that is arch, in *Faded Leaves* her eyes. But Marguerite's is no commonplace archness, merely flirtatious and provocative. Arnold interprets it as the outward sign of an inward grace:

> The lovely lips, with their arch smile that tells
> The unconquered joy in which her spirit dwells.

This joyous spirit makes her voice too 'buoyant as morning'. And in *Euphrosyne* (assuming this to be one of the Marguerite poems) Arnold concludes sadly that what he had fancied to be love for himself was 'bliss within'—sheer creative love of life, one of the supreme virtues of the spirit.

Marguerite was indeed no beautiful nonentity, Browning's 'pretty woman', her beauty her sole duty. Beneath that dazzling smile and in those impetuous blue eyes Arnold saw 'an angelic gravity', while the mockery (perhaps) becomes more significant as a 'deep disdain'. Arnold is here suggesting a certain intellectual quality that is confirmed elsewhere. The 1852 title of the fifth *Switzerland* poem was 'To Marguerite, In returning a volume of the Letters of Ortis',[1] which indicates a sharing of cultural interests. The two parts of the poem *Isolation* (of which the 'Ortis' poem later became the second half) have an intellectual content inappropriate to a river-girl. It is amusing (or perhaps it is sad) to learn that Arnold's second choice was different in this respect. Alan Harris[2] tells us that Arnold said of Frances Lucy that she was 'entirely free from taint of letters'.

Thus Marguerite seems to have been a young woman with whom a brilliant young man from Balliol, private secretary to Lord

---

[1] The identity of 'Ortis', the apparent writer of this 'volume of letters', for a time eluded me, but the invaluable *Larousse* brought him to light. He is not a writer but (like poor Enoch Soames) a character in a novel. The book Marguerite lent Arnold was a novel in epistolary form by the Italian poet Ugo Foscolo (1778–1827), and its title was *Ultime lettere di Jacopo Ortis*. It might seem that Arnold did not read beyond the title, and overlooked the real author, but Marguerite clearly knew that the book (which is said to be one of the best specimens of modern Italian prose) was suitable reading for a man of culture.

[2] 'Matthew Arnold, the Unknown Years', *The Nineteenth Century*, April 1933.

Lansdowne, could spend a summer or two without wasting his time, and Arnold was, up to a point, in love. Why then did the adventure come to an end so quickly, and Arnold content himself with writing out his heart in a handful of what Mr Blunden calls 'elegies of love'? The principal reason was doubtless that the son of Doctor Arnold was prudent and acute enough to analyse the difference between 'love' and 'being in love'. In other words, as I have already suggested, he was never very serious about the affair. Harris, in the article quoted above, suggests that he availed himself of the artist's freedom to use experience and then end it. (But was Arnold ever an 'artist' in this sense of being above the law?)

But in the poems he does give a number of specific reasons why he and Marguerite had to part. The reasons are not always consistent. At one point she is faithless, at another he has ceased to love her. More intriguing is his assertion that what comes between them is that they have had 'a different past'. He himself has been—one supposes, though with the Victorians it was not a thing that mattered —free from sex-entanglements, while Marguerite's lips have been prest 'to the lips, ah! of others', and others, 'ere I was', have been strained to her breast. How far we are to press these terms it is impossible to say, but certainly not to the point of supposing (as one writer has done) that Marguerite was a prostitute, though Arnold himself was ungallant enough to imagine, in the poem written ten years later, that she might by that time have dissipated her sweetness in rouge and riotous laughter, or, worse still, grown old and ugly. He ends this belated and embittered poem with the line,

<blockquote>And Marguerite I shall see no more—</blockquote>

which may have been a promise long ago exacted by Fanny Lucy.

Of Frances Lucy Wightman, Arnold's second love and his wife as soon as he could afford to marry, we know very little, though if we have read Isobel Macdonald's novel, *The Buried Life*, we may imagine we know a good deal.[1] There are two 'love-poems' which speak a different language from that of *Switzerland* and *Faded Leaves*.

[1] The commentators on Marguerite ignore Miss Wightman altogether.

There the tone throughout is lightly passionate, mock-despairing, with philosophic comments too profound for the situation. In *Calais Sands* and *Dover Beach* there is a new note of seriousness and unqualified tenderness. Both poems appeared first in the *New Poems* of 1867, though the MS. of *Calais Sands* is headed 'August 1850'. The febrile excitement to which we have become accustomed is quite absent from *Calais Sands,* and *Dover Beach* provides a lovely picture of married love: the poet, looking out on the calm, moonlit straits, speaks over his shoulder to his wife— 'Come to the window'. He interprets for her, in his way, the sound of the waves upon the beach, hearing 'the eternal note of sadness' and comparing it with the ebbing of 'the Sea of Faith'. He lets the mood oppress him, making him see life as a loveless, joyless confusion of struggle and flight, with but one refuge—

> Ah, love, let us be true
> To one another!

The Victorians were specialists (for good and ill) in the husband-wife relation.

There are a few more poems that may be taken as belonging, less exclusively, to the category we are examining. *The Buried Life* is in the main a further outpouring of Arnold's sense of personal isolation and the purposelessness of life, but his thoughts are allowed to have their origin in a lovers' altercation—'Light flows our war of mocking words. . . .' The gay opponent may have been either of Arnold's two 'loves', but this opening reads like a continuation of the primary theme. However, when he comes to show the mystic efficacy of love the reference must be to something that he has now learnt to know, something more peaceful and permanent than the emotions of the Marguerite adventure. The phrase, 'but this is rare', suggests that love was not a major influence in Arnold's life: it is much that he should have found in it even a temporary entry to the world of mystic enlightenment.

Finally there are the companion poems, *Euphrosyne* and *Urania*. I have already accepted the first of these as a consequence of Arnold's experience with Marguerite, the opening line, 'I must not say that thou wast true', being a well-established motif in her brief history, and the conclusion, the recognition of the vital happiness that looked so much like love, affording a final analysis of her positive quality. *Urania*, though doubtless suggested by the amused scorn in Marguerite's 'lovely eyes', is perhaps intended to represent the poet's views on women generally, rather than on one special woman—I hope to return to this point.

I ought to say that H. W. Garrod and Sir Edmund Chambers, who are exceedingly good and understanding about the love-poems, wish (like M. Bonnerot) to include among them—or at least to see the influence of Marguerite in—a number of other poems: *The Forsaken Merman, Tristram and Iseult, Obermann, The Youth of Nature* and *The Youth of Man*. Garrod indeed hears Marguerite's footsteps everywhere, and regards 1847-9 as a critical period in Arnold's life, with lasting effects. This may be so, but I am not inclined to take Marguerite so seriously.

It is a homespun, an earth-bound love that is presented with such attractive intimacy in these poems. There is here no lurid passion like that of the *Sonnets*, nor any touch of the fine abandon of Burns, the romantic etherealism of Shelley, the angel-worship of Browning and Patmore. There *is* intense feeling in the *Switzerland* and *Faded Leaves* poems, but the feeling is inspired not by Marguerite but by the poet's painful sense of his own inability to enter fully into the world of love. There was something half Puritan in his breeding, and he was ruled by intellectualism; these kept him from the sheer joyousness of love. Whether by nature or by training, he was incapable of the anguish of the cry—

> Dear as remembered kisses after death,

or of comprehending the passion, profound though half-humorous, of Browning's brag—

> A face to lose youth for, to occupy age
> With the dream of, meet death with . . .

Yet these love-poems are beautiful and delicate and above all moving. I find nothing so close, familiar, human till I come to Hardy's *Poems of 1912-13* and the ghost-poems of de la Mare. There is, of course, in both these poets a tragic intensity never approached by Arnold, but when Hardy writes,

> It was your way, my dear,
> To vanish without a word,

or de la Mare murmurs,

> O ghost, draw nearer,

we may feel the same intimate, human response as in Arnold's pleading—

> While yet the night is chill,
> Upon night's barren, stormy flow,
> Stay with me, Marguerite, still!

or,

> Again I see my bliss at hand,
> The town, the lake are here;
> My Marguerite smiles upon the strand
> Unaltered with the year.

It is a purely human love, accessible to all men save those whom Coleridge calls 'the Sensual and the Proud', yet still the love through which the common man most readily achieves divinity, if only for a moment; the love about which Coventry Patmore said,

> Love wakes men, once a lifetime each.
> They lift their heavy lids, and look,
> And lo, what one sweet page may teach
> They read with joy, then shut the book.

And then, having breathed all this faint disparagement, I turn to that poem, which though appearing, like *A Memory Picture*, in the 1849 volume, seems to speak from far other depths. This is *The Voice*, which both Garrod and Chambers place with the Marguerite poems. I suppose it may belong with them, though there Marguerite's

voice has anything but 'melancholy tones'. (The poet, calling them
also 'lute-like', says they 'blew a thrilling summons': it is hardly
necessary to point out that a lute is not blown—can Arnold have
meant to write 'flute'?) The poem is baffling, and does not quite
convince. I get an impression of artificiality from the first stanza,
which is an obvious imitation of Shelley; the second begins like
Shelley but soon turns to Tennyson. And then, with startling
suddenness, the verse becomes completely personal and sincere, and
breaks in a passionate and imaginative utterance unheard in any of
the other poems:

> O unforgotten voice, thy accents come
> Like wanderers from the world's extremity
> Unto their ancient home.

(If, like Coleridge, I had come upon these lines 'running wild in the
desert' I should have 'screamed out'—not 'Wordsworth' but 'Walter
de la Mare!') And the third stanza continues the passionate strain to
the point where the poet declares that the 'voice'

> Made my tost heart its very life-blood spill,
>   Yet could not break it,

nor shake his will.

If this is Marguerite, then she stirred Arnold more deeply than
she has seemed from the other poems to have done. There are
indications (and not only in the 'long-distant years'[1] which Arnold
originally wrote, the alteration to 'the bygone year' not being made
till 1877) that *The Voice* may be an echo of an earlier love. Or is it,
as the build-up might suggest, the one love-poem based on a purely
imaginative experience?

In discussing Arnold's qualities as an artist I omitted the love-
poems. This was not because they are unworthy of mention in this
respect. On the contrary, some of his most delightful brush-work is
to be found here. Consider the second poem of the *Switzerland*

---

[1] Chambers discounts this expression, saying it would take us back to his
boyhood, but it need not mean more than six or seven years.

sequence, called *Parting*. The verse is varied with consummate skill. The poem opens in a swift short dactylic metre, figuring the poet's distraught mind and the rushing wind that matches it. Suddenly this is quietened to a lovely stanza in iambic couplets:

> But on the stairs what voice is this I hear,
> Buoyant as morning, and as morning clear?
> Say, has some wet, bird-haunted English lawn
> Lent it the music of its trees at dawn?

His fevered heart takes charge again in the staccato measure, till the soothing pentameters again bring relief:

> But who is this, by the half-opened door,
> Whose figure casts a shadow on the floor?
> The sweet blue eyes—the soft ash-coloured hair . . .

But the torrent of the poet's agitation is only momentarily held up by these two still pools of beauty, and the poem continues in turbulent metrical waves to its end in a prayer to Nature for calm amid

> the stir of the forces
> Whence issued the world.

The next poem, *A Farewell*, is unconscionably long for its subject (Arnold might have learnt from Browning's supreme succinctness in *The Lost Mistress*, published a few years earlier), but it also has some perfectly fashioned phrases—

> I too have longed for trenchant force
> And will like a dividing spear;

though the beautiful sound-picture,

> The hush among the shining stars,
> The calm upon the moonlit sea,

recalls, to its own disadvantage, the matchless distich of Arnold's master:

> The silence that is in the starry sky,
> The sleep that is among the lonely hills.

The other poem where form and feeling, conception and execution, are superlatively fused is the second of the *Isolation* poems,
number 5 of the *Switzerland* series. Whether or not Arnold is right
in seeing the individuals who make up humanity as completely cut
off from vital communication with one another, the extended
figure by which he represents this condition is beyond criticism, and
is embodied in a quite flawless form of words: the 'sea of life' in
which each being is 'enisled', the 'echoing straits' that separate the
'islands' except when 'on starry nights the nightingales divinely sing',
when 'a longing like despair' almost brings about the miracle of
union, but desire is vain against the fate that has decreed their
severance,

> And bade between their shores to be
> The unplumbed, salt, estranging sea.

Not Keats himself could have made a better selection of epithets
than those last three, and the whole poem is a masterpiece.

All these poems are brilliantly made, half of them in iambic
tetrameter with alternate rhymes, but the rest in a variety of stanza
forms, all well handled. I have spoken of the blank verse of *The
Dream* (outside the two named groups), where Arnold paints, in
verse that moves swiftly and easily, a vividly coloured picture of the
banks of the river down which he and 'Martin' are sailing in the
dream. The verse slows down a little, meditatively, as they see
Marguerite and 'Olivia'[1] appear on the balcony of the cottage.
With a sudden leap the verse, like the boat, hurries on again till it
drops to stillness in the final line, where the only variation from
natural speech-order conveys a sense of menace:

> us burning plains,
> Bristled with cities, us the sea received.

The interposition of an explanatory line in a revision thirty years
later seems unnecessary. Having written in 1853

[1] Is there any reason why Martin and Olivia should not have been Clough and
Blanche Smith?

> One moment, on the rapid's top, our boat
> Hung poised—and then the darting river of Life,
> Loud thundering, bore us by,

he was in 1881 not content to let the sudden metaphor effect its own justification, and between the second and third of these lines inserted

> (Such now methought it was) the river of Life . . .

This is unobjectionable, and does not detract from the fine swift unity, the perfect integralness, with which the poem is composed, but the bolder, blunter statement was better.

This sheaf of poems, a score or so in all, contains some of Arnold's most admirable writing. The versification of the earliest of all, the *Memory Picture*, is a little amateurish, trivial, but every other poem shows the hand of a master. Other love-poem sequences written in the middle decades of the century were Browning's *James Lee's Wife*, Tennyson's *Maud*, and Meredith's *Modern Love*. Of the four groups, Browning's excels in varied psychological interest, Meredith's in huge intellectual power and imagery. *Maud* tells a melodramatic story with matchless technical brilliance, but only rises to beauty in the supreme lyric, 'Come into the garden, Maud'. For consistent poetical charm the Arnold poems hold their own.

F

CHAPTER IV

Some other Poems

The titles, in order of publication:

THIS selection of twenty-seven poems represents, with the love-poems (and I ought to add the *Shakespeare* sonnet, *Requiescat* and *Palladium*), my personal choice, except for *Merope*, which is included because I feel it deserves rather more attention than it has generally received.

(a) *Three 'Free Verse' Poems*

Until the coming of the new verse, poets had looked upon form as wheels or wings, not as shackles, and—apart from Whitman, who achieved something very like poetry by surrendering himself to certain gigantic and lawless rhythms—had seldom dreamed of letting go the inspiration and lifting power of metre and regular

verse. Arnold made more use of free verse than any other poet
before 1914, and two of his greatest poems, *Dover Beach* and *The
Future*, achieve supreme success under the handicap of apparent
formlessness. Once, in *The Strayed Reveller*, the title poem of the
volume with which 'A' broke upon a small and surprised audience,
he brings off his effect by the illegitimate device of printing prose
unashamedly as verse. It is patent deceit to divide into verses a
passage like this:

> Quick I passed, following the wood-cutter's cart-
> track down the dark valley; I saw on my left, through
> the beeches, thy palace, Goddess, smokeless, empty.
> Trembling, I entered; beheld the court all silent,
> the lions sleeping, on the altar this bowl.

Or like this:

> Sitting in his cart he makes his meal; before him,
> for long miles, alive with bright green lizards and
> the springing bustard fowl, the track, a straight
> black line, furrows the rich soil; here and there
> clusters of lonely mounds topped with rough-hewn,
> grey, rain-bleared statues, overpeer the sunny waste.

The construction, with its common-place word-order and its
absence of rhythm (Saintsbury claimed to have found snatches of
blank verse), is that of plain prose.

But the poem had begun like this:

> Faster, faster,
> O Circe, Goddess,
> Let the wild, thronging train,
> The bright procession
> Of eddying forms
> Sweep through my soul!

And here, in some quite inexplicable way, we have the transporting
effect of rhythmic form. True, we are almost immediately brought

up by the stilted phrase, 'thy right arm leaned up against the column there'; but the initial momentum carries us on and over this snag in the stream and enables, indeed compels us to accept the swift succession of little prose paragraphs as if they were metrical stanzas. The fact is that Arnold, inspired by his Homeric theme, has let the substance of his imagination stream forth with Homeric directness, speed taking the place of metre, and so produced a poem unique in English.

Though evidently written at white heat, and remaining (a thing unusual with Arnold) unaltered through all the editions, the poem is exquisitely fashioned, with its three persons playing perfectly balanced parts. The main action—i.e. utterance—is given to the venturesome youth who, under the influence of the magic liquor, holds forth to the goddess and the more illustrious Wanderer. He passes before them a panorama of life, first in its ideal form as designed by the gods, then from a worm's-eye view that sees only the defects, and finally through his own eyes, which, at moments when clarified by happiness, had penetrated through the crust of actuality to the visionary beauty beyond.

> But I, Ulysses,
> Sitting on the warm steps,
> Looking over the valley,
> All day long, have seen,
> Without pain, without labour,
> Sometimes a wild-haired Maenad—
> Sometimes a Faun with torches—
> And sometimes, for a moment,
> Passing through the dark stems
> Flowing-robed, the beloved,
> The desired, the divine,
> Beloved Iacchus.

The serene outlook did not return till that very late poem, *Thyrsis*, and then of course in a more mature, more creative form.

Dover Beach is a far greater poem than *The Strayed Reveller*. Though short, it has a massive bulk contrasted with the crystal

trickle of the earlier poem. It is only 'free' in the sense that lines and
stanzas are of uneven length: it is as firmly bound by rhyme and
inner tension as the *Immortality* ode. Almost half the lines are in the
measure that speaks from and to the profoundest depths of the
English genius—iambic pentameter: note how we are led up to it
at the beginning of the poem, with three feet, four feet, and then a
block of decasyllabics. After this the metre swings from short to
long in a pattern which is felt to be inevitable, until it closes in the
heavy finality of the line—'Where ignorant armies clash by night'.
On the way it has included one of the finest passages in all Arnold,
the paragraph beginning, 'The Sea of Faith' (quoted in the last
chapter). Unlike the *Reveller*, the poem provoked Arnold to much
revision of detail, as Tinker and Lowry show in their fascinating
notes. Thus, over the lines,

> Where the sea meets the moon-blanched land,
> Listen! you hear the grating roar
> Of pebbles which the waves draw back . . .

in the various editions he rang the changes on 'sea' and 'ebb', 'land'
and 'sand', 'draw' and 'suck'. One is not disposed to quarrel with a
final result so splendid, otherwise one might have said that 'sand'
and 'suck' give the clearer picture.

I have commented elsewhere on what seems to me the discord
between the lovely appeal, 'Ah love, let us be true to one another',
and the sordid assertion that the world has 'neither joy nor love'.
I observe that Mr Jump, with gloating approval of the 'beat'
philosophy, concludes that this is Arnold's greatest poem, while
from another angle Humphrey House felt here 'an unbalanced
exaggeration of domestic virtues'. Mr Kingsmill (whose book,
though full of niggles, shows a sound appreciation of Arnold's
poetry) sets the blind pessimism of the world without joy or love
against a sentence from Arnold's own *God and the Bible*: 'Jesus hits
the plain natural truth that human life is a blessing and a benefit.'

But accepting this poet's desperate outlook, we must admit that
the use of the 'eternal note of sadness' in the 'melancholy long

withdrawing roar' of the sucking waves is a marvellous way of
figuring the retreat of the 'sea of faith', and that the appearance of a
world where conflict (though in truth pleasantly varied with
friendship and co-operation) is undoubtedly wide-spread, is again
brilliantly presented in the image of

> a darkling plain
> Swept with confused alarms of struggle and flight
> Where ignorant armies clash by night—

so brilliantly, indeed, that I am not sure that Arnold did not keep
the image more for its brilliance than for its truth.

The third of these free-verse poems is the greatest, indeed the
greatest of all Arnold's poems other than *The Scholar-Gipsy* and
Thyrsis. *The Future* is more nobly creative than *Dover Beach*. In that
poem, after the perfect descriptive opening and the pious allusion to
Sophocles, we get the great conception of the Sea of Faith and then
the depressing—realistic if you see it so, but surely depressing—
conclusion as to the present state of the world. This one, basing
itself on the common figure of time as a river, comprehends a
majestic retrospect of the history of man from its early beginnings—

> The tribes who then roamed on her breast,
> Her vigorous, primitive sons—

to a sublime vision of man's ultimate destiny, an infinite and eternal
peace; not a negative, empty peace, but one filled with those
excellences—freedom and adventure, wonder and dream—that the
word sea connotes.

It has been suggested that Arnold changes his perspective for the
conclusion of the poem from mankind to the individual man. But
unless you are a materialist it is not impossible to see the human
species attaining an end—or a next stage—in a purely spiritual
development which might be indicated in Arnold's picture of
movement towards a vital eternity.

Mr Kingsmill has tried to spoil the poem by casting historical doubt on the parts played by Rebecca and Moses. As well try to flaw Marvell's cameo of King Charles—

> He nothing common did or mean
> Upon that memorable scene,
> > But bowed his comely head
> > Down, as upon a bed—

by reference to his shortcomings as a constitutional monarch.

However, it is not the theme or the philosophy that gives *The Future* its transcendent quality, but (paradoxically) its form. Without rhyme, and with more metrical variety than *Dover Beach*, every line falls into its place with complete inevitability. From the opening lines—which I suggest should be read without stop at the end of the first line but with a definite pause at the end of the second:

A wanderer is man from his birth he was born in a ship. . . .
On the breast of the river of Time—

the 'auditory imagination' sways to and fro, rising and falling and carrying the reader on great waves of aesthetic emotion, following the stages of Arnold's developing conception, until, after the prelusive couplet,

> But what was before us we know not,
> And we know not what shall succeed,

opening the mind to wonder and expectation, we ascend to the height of the final vision, embodied in the almost Miltonic verse-paragraph:

> And the width of the waters, the hush
> Of the grey expanse where he floats,
> Freshening its current and spotted with foam
> As it draws to the Ocean, may strike
> Peace to the soul of the man on its breast—
> As the pale waste widens around him,
> As the banks fade dimmer away,
> As the stars come out, and the night-wind
> Brings up the stream
> Murmurs and scents of the infinite sea.

How the shortened penultimate line draws back in preparation for the last luminous phrase, each of its three dactyls based on a beautiful word with rich associative qualities. Though, as I have said, the reference can and ought to be the destiny of mankind, it can certainly have an individual and personal meaning too, and I like to imagine myself (like Hardy asking for the three poems on his death-bed) finding it easier to die with that last paragraph of *The Future* sounding in my ears.

The poem, like the *Reveller,* but by a greater miracle to a loftier end, was born with the integrity of a single thought, complete with diction and form, and required no revision.

(b) *Two Dramatic Poems*

From these winged lyrics let us turn to the heavier but not negligible verse dramas. I think Browning showed better taste in persuading Arnold to reprint *Empedocles on Etna* than in withdrawing his own early poem, *Pauline*, though the Browning work with which *Empedocles* asks to be compared is *Paracelsus*. As a verse-play it is not attractive, and is only held together by the songs of Callicles. Some of these Arnold published separately, but they are much more effective in their proper place: the device of making the music of song and harp come up through the silence 'from below' is excellent. Pausanias is a dull dog, and his conversations with Callicles and Empedocles are cast in blank verse that only comes to life when the scenery of the valley is being described. I have spoken of the entire lack of grace in the stanza-form that Arnold chose for the long didactic speech Empedocles makes for the benefit of Pausanias, but its substance is not unsound, and leads up to a thought which Arnold often forgot (if he had borne it in mind the first part of my first chapter would have been unnecessary):

> Is it so small a thing
> To have enjoyed the sun,
> To have lived light in the spring,
> To have loved, to have thought, to have done?

And infers that since there is this much of good in life on earth it is unnecessary to postulate another life in compensation. Empedocles' final word to Pausanias is—Neither fear nor despair, but live in reasonable hope. And Callicles' quaint song of the 'two bright and aged snakes' comes up to suggest the happiness of secluded quiet.

The second act is a far finer piece of work. It is divided between Empedocles, who speaks in soliloquy, and Callicles, who twice relieves the argument with his songs and sings a final comment on what Empedocles has said and done. (He has played, not quite effectually, the part of David to Saul.) From Empedocles' long soliloquy, couched partly in blank verse of moderate quality and partly in free verse, we gather that he realises that his pessimism (not unrelieved, as we have seen) is due to a personal 'deadness to life and joy'. (So Arnold had confessed to Clough his 'weakness, coldness, languor of spirit'.) But though he has been neither the slave of sense nor master of his soul, yet he can say,

> I have loved no darkness,
> Sophisticated no truth,
> Nursed no delusion,
> Allowed no fear.

And so, with the cloud mounting off his soul, he not so much commits suicide as gives himself to the elements. And Callicles' musical commentary repeats on a larger scale the joyous vision of the *Reveller*:

> What forms are these coming . . .
> What sweet-breathing presence?
>
> 'Tis Apollo comes leading
> His choir, the Nine.
> The leader is fairest
> But all are divine . . .
>
> First hymn they the Father
> Of all things; and then,
> The rest of immortals,
> The action of men.

> The day in his hotness,
> The strife with the palm;
> The night in her silence,
> The stars in their calm.

Comparison with *Paracelsus* is inevitable. *Empedocles* was published in 1852, when Arnold was thirty, *Paracelsus* in 1835 when Browning was twenty-three, each poet having previously published one work. Arnold took a Greek philosopher as his mouthpiece, Browning a mediaeval scholar-mystic, and neither made much use of the teachings of his original. Arnold gives Empedocles stoical ethics and Lucretian views of nature. Structurally, *Empedocles* is a trifle beside the majestic scheme of *Paracelsus*, but in philosophical content it holds its ground, though there is a mystical element in Paracelsus's thinking which goes further than the purely intellectual processes of the Greek. In each case the truths arrived at are given in a dying speech, that of Empedocles before he plunges into the crater, that of Paracelsus as he lies on his death-bed. Paracelsus's conclusion is the nobler in its insistence on love as the vital spirit of life. Empedocles, in both parts of his exposition, dwells markedly on the priority of mind: 'Mind is the spell which governs earth and heaven', and later—

> But mind? . . .
> But mind, but thought—
> If these have been the master part of us,
> Where will *they* find their parent element?

Paracelsus had early declared, 'God, thou art *Mind*', to be answered by Festus, 'God, thou art love! I build my faith on that', and in his dying speech Paracelsus admits,

> I learned my own deep error; love's undoing
> Taught me the worth of love.

Browning's poem covers vaster areas of speculation, as well as twenty-nine years of dramatic action, while Arnold is content with a few static hours of self-analysis, but within its limits *Empedocles on*

Etna has good things to say, and says them well. The songs of Callicles are more memorable than those that occur in *Paracelsus*, and Mr Eliot's opinion is that *Empedocles* is 'one of the finest academic poems ever written'.

Merope, on the other hand, is regarded as a failure, and Trilling calls it 'ridiculous'. It certainly has little entertainment value, but what poetic play of the nineteenth century has? It will naturally not bear comparison with the Greek tragedies, these having been written by men of supreme dramatic and poetic genius, but it is a true Greek play for all that. The blank verse is generally not more than competent and is sometimes quite wooden, but in places where strong feeling is present it rises to a high level.[1] The chorus is a good Greek chorus, and its longer utterances (sometimes too long) are mostly written in Arnold's favourite short *Rugby Chapel* line, but only once does this achieve beauty of metre and diction (lines 1596-1683).

As with the older Greek plays, the action of *Merope* implies a knowledge of the earlier history of the families concerned, and this Arnold supplies in his introduction, but all that is really necessary is to know that Polyphontes, now King of Messenia, has murdered the previous king, Cresphontes, and forcibly married his widow, Merope. Though this was many years ago, Merope has never forgiven Polyphontes, and refuses to listen to his pleadings for amity. Merope and Cresphontes had had three sons, two of whom had been murdered with their father, but the third, Aepytus, had escaped, and has now returned to Messenia with a view to avenging his father's death. Being in disguise, he is able to pretend that he is a messenger come to tell of Aepytus's death. He meets Polyphontes and describes to him how Aepytus had met his death by drowning. But Arcas, an old retainer of Merope's, has a different tale, explaining to Merope that Aepytus is dead by treachery, having been killed, together with his guardian, Laias, by a hunting companion bribed to commit the murder. Merope believes that the messenger (really her son) who had told the first tale is a spy, and determines to

---

[1] E.g. lines 89-109, 197-277, 291-305, 786-844, 1288-1330.

kill him. This she is just prevented from doing by Arcas, and mother and son are brought together. Aepytus now tells his mother of his projected vengeance on Polyphontes, and though she is against bloodshed, after a long and skilfully conducted debate between Merope, Aepytus and Laias (brother of the late King), she agrees, and Aepytus goes to carry out his deed. Polyphontes makes a last appeal to Merope to forgive and forget, but she again refuses, Polyphontes retires and is presently carried in dead, Aepytus being left to assume the sovereignty of Messenia.

There has been some argument about the respective roles of Merope and Polyphontes. Merope is the titular heroine, but Polyphontes is declared more attractive. I think this is an error, due to his plausible tongue, exactly as with Claudius. Only in *Hamlet*, Claudius's soft speeches beguile and captivate the wife he has won by murder; in Arnold's play Merope is utterly impervious to Polyphontes' blandishments and rebuffs him again and again. At one point, after a particularly pathetic appeal by Polyphontes, Merope's reply (line 1729—) provokes the exclamation, 'What a fury the woman is!'. But consideration shows that she is merely refusing to admit that the passage of time can obliterate the fact of murder. This man murdered her husband and forced her to marry him: he has behaved nicely ever since, but he is still the murderer of her husband and still holds her in forced wedlock; no degree of sentimental rhetoric can do away with those facts. The admiration his pathetic speeches have earned for him is on a par with the other mistaken notion that Satan's courage ought to make us forget that Milton intended him for the spirit of evil.

Merope is the splendid, strong type of Greek heroine, like Antigone and Electra, but she is given a Christian, Arnoldian dislike of bloodshed. Even though her loyalty to her husband's memory is absolute, and she cannot forget the cry of her children—

The Fury to them,
Fresh from their father draws near.
Ah, bloody axe! dizzy blows!

yet she insists that she wants reparation 'without blood'.

> An avenger I ask not—send me my son!
> Can vengeance give me back the murdered?

Her grief at the (false) news that Aepytus is dead, and her belief that the tale of his death by drowning had been inspired by Polyphontes, the instigator of the attack, drives her to the otherwise inconsistent action of trying to kill the 'messenger'. She returns to her real self after her reunion with her son, for when he tells her he has come back for revenge she exclaims, 'Ah! . . . revenge! That word it kills me!' She continues to argue against bloodshed, and though she will not yield to Polyphontes she asserts her belief in his respect for her and his intention to rule peacefully, but at last gives way to the insistent arguments of Aepytus and Laias, put by Arnold in a series of clear and dramatic speeches. Having agreed, she continues to play her part of angry repulsion of Polyphontes' last appeal, and sends him to his death at the hands of Aepytus.

Aristotle would perhaps not have rated *Merope* high, as there is no tragic hero: Polyphontes' crime is too serious to be called a 'flaw', and the central scene, containing most of the play's tension and suspense, is between Merope and her son. Yet the usurping king's seductiveness is such that his death does excite a degree of 'pity and terror'.

Merope is a fine Greek matron, more human than some of her ancient prototypes, introspective, and more acceptable to the modern mind. Placed against Polyphontes' consistent graciousness, her figure gives the play an aspect of genuine interest, and I can only account for Trilling's contempt by supposing him to have come to it after a rich diet of American paper-backs.

(c) *Two Elegies*

Memorial Verses, April 1850, is an exquisite miniature of criticism. The person elegised is Wordsworth, but brilliant thumb-nail estimates of Goethe and Byron are given in order to throw up the

central figure by way of contrast, just one element in the genius of
each being named, 'Goethe's sage mind and Byron's force'. For
Wordsworth, Arnold selects four prime qualities—his power to
bring us into sympathetic touch with nature, his 'healing power',
his power of quickening the feelings, and, above all, his power of
making us realise the unimportance of the finite, the all-importance
of the infinite:

> The cloud of mortal destiny . . .
> . . . who, like him, will put it by?

This is, indeed, quintessential Wordsworth, and we see how much
better it is for a poet to put what he feels about another poet into a
poem than into critical prose. The essay on *Wordsworth*, written
nearly thirty years after the *Verses*, is a sound piece of work, done
without enthusiasm. Arnold tells us he places Wordsworth third in
English poetry, after Shakespeare and Milton, but we should not
have surmised this from the rest of the essay. He thinks little of
The Prelude, nothing of *The Excursion*, is doubtful about the
'intimations' of the *Ode* (which is otherwise 'declamatory'), and
does not mention the *Tintern Abbey* lines, the *Lucy* poems, or the
great sonnets. Still, he dwells emphatically on the power of joy in
Wordsworth's poetry, so that we know he had the root of the matter
in him.

The poem of 1850 is quite perfect as a work of art. It is exactly
the right length, and has not an excessive line or one out of place.
The opening lines have a classic economy and force:

> Goethe in Weimar sleeps, and Greece
> Long since saw Byron's struggles cease.
> But one such death remained to come:
> The last poetic voice is dumb—
> We stand today by Wordsworth's tomb.

Then follow a short verse paragraph on Byron, a rather longer one
on Goethe, and the main pronouncement on Wordsworth. Note
the skilful variation of the lines that introduce the three sections:

When Byron's eyes were shut in death . . .

When Goethe's death was told, we said . . .

And Wordsworth!—Ah! pale ghosts, rejoice!

Having told us wherein Wordsworth excelled, he comes back, in a fifth paragraph, to the comparison with Byron and Goethe—their qualities may repeat themselves in others, but Wordsworth was and will remain unique. And he says this again in the lovely singing conclusion—

> Keep fresh the grass upon his grave,
> O Rotha, with thy living wave!
> Sing him thy best! for few or none
> Hears thy voice right, now he is gone—

no one has ever, like Wordsworth, brought the spirit of man into intimate, vitalising touch with the spirit of nature.

The octosyllabic couplet is handled faultlessly, often with epigrammatic precision, yet with ease and informality. How differently, ineffectively, prosily is the same measure used in the other 'critical' poem, *Epilogue to Lessing's Laocoon*, which maunders along, pleasantly enough, to a sound if not ineluctable conclusion.

The metre—what R. H. Hutton called the 'recitative'—of *Rugby Chapel* is more plainly that of a dirge. The poem was written in November and establishes its tone with the first few words—'Coldly, sadly descends the evening'. The looser measure, trochaic-dactylic, unrhymed, lends itself to an undisciplined outpouring of feeling very different from the tight artistry of the *Memorial Verses*, and the central bulk of the poem might with advantage have been cut to a third of its length: the substance of Arnold's tribute to his father would have remained unweakened by the omission of lines 58-133, where the lugubrious imagery reflects the son rather than the father, though it would be a pity to lose the passage which declares that a few strive to snatch something from oblivion, 'nor all glut the devouring grave'.[1] The spirit of the poem is unusually religious:

[1] cf *Paradise Lost*, III. 259, 'and with his carcase glut the grave.'

Arnold had waited fifteen years after his father's death, by which time he not only had his subject in perspective but had moved out of the indifferentism of his early middle years. Apart from the theistic ending, he is able, without returning to orthodoxy, to voice the exhilarating belief that the great headmaster may still, after death, be exercising his splendid gifts:

> Somewhere, surely, afar,
> In the sounding labour-house vast
> Of being, is practised that strength,
> Zealous, beneficent, firm—

(one of Arnold's favourite triple adjective groupings). The 'fifteen years' was not a deliberately chosen period: Arnold told his mother he had been moved to write the poem by an attack on his father by Fitzjames Stephen. (A more seemly reply than that made by Browning to the other 'Fitz'!)

(d) *Ten Poems on Life*

Resignation is one of those poems—Wordsworth provides a number—which have an added dimension for readers who know the Lake District. (I have never been able to decide whether the fact detracts from the absolute value of a poem.) This poem falls into five parts, and the second part is a recollection, shared with his sister Jane, whom he calls Fausta, of a walk they had done in 1833 (ten years previously) with a party led by Thomas Arnold. As Arnold says in his note, those 'familiar with the English Lake country' will be able to trace the walk, and—one may add—will take enormous pleasure in doing so. Setting out from the Nag's Head on Thirlmere (no longer an inn alas!) the party will have crossed, not Thirlmere itself, which at that time did not extend so far (Manchester's thirst being then less unassuageable), but a 'rude stone bridge' over the Wyth Burn at a point now submerged. Then they climbed Armboth Fell and descended on 'the farms' at Watendlath. So far Arnold's note takes us, but the party now followed

Watendlath Beck down to the lake and 'the noisy town' of Keswick. Presently we are told that they reached the sea. Messrs Tinker and Lowry, writing from America, and M. Bonnerot, from France, surmise that Arnold must mean the lake, Derwentwater. But it is clear that the tireless young walkers, having done the eight or nine miles from the Nag's Head to Keswick, now went on along the road beside Bassenthwaite—'many a mile of dusty way'—to Cockermouth, and eventually reached 'the wide glimmering sea' somewhere between Maryport and Workington, having covered some thirty miles in the day, a very respectable 'hike', as we should have called it twenty-five years ago when people still did such things.

The relevance of the walk to the argument of the poem is not obvious (I cannot believe, with M. Bonnerot, that the walk is an image of life—Arnold was not wont at that time to present life's progress in such favourable terms), but perhaps (since the walk is being partly repeated ten years later) enforces one of the poem's ideas, that the world does not change, however much man may do so. The gypsies they see on the second walk are used to emphasise the conception of the changelessness of life. The first part of the poem, preceding the itinerary, distinguishes between two types of people, the ambitious, the fierce strivers after the goal of completed action, and those who are 'resigned' to accepting life as it comes. 'Fausta' is recommended to be one of these 'milder natures'.

In the fourth section, the heart of the poem and beautifully written, Arnold expounds the poet's contemplative vision. The poet has done and suffered, but rejects action and suffering as imperfect modes of life. Subordinating his personal life, he surveys mankind and nature. He sees man doing great deeds and achieving great triumphs, but does not envy them. Instead, he gazes quietly over the awakening earth—

> Before him he sees life unroll,
> A placid and continuous whole—

and knows that the secret of the universal life is a peaceful continuity outlasting death. This is the life which the poet, with his 'sad

G

lucidity of soul', craves, and it was hinted at in the first section. The idea seems to be a kind of entering into the life of the time-spirit, or earth spirit. Returning to the first theme he again urges on Fausta 'quiet and a fearless mind', gently reproaching her for letting her heart be busy about the vanity of human cares. The poet, secure in his vision, may appear weak and foolish to the world, but he sees in each moment the birth of life and death. Action blinds us and carries us no further, but nature teaches us 'to bear rather than rejoice'.

If I have done any sort of justice to the argument it will be obvious that this poem is not the profound philosophical achievement some critics would have it, but it is full of delectable things. It is an 'occasional' poem, probably composed in Arnold's early twenties, with his sister for primary and admiring audience. I value it more for its beauty than for its message, and find it chiefly notable for the intensely felt memories of the Lakeland walk and the panoramic vision, which inspired Arnold to some of his loveliest writing, and at one place to a pastoral scene that consciously emulates *L'Allegro*.

Consolation, much less ambitious, a brevity in the briefest of unrhymed metres cast in miniature five-line stanzas, has had some fun poked at it but is a genuine artistic achievement. Setting the scene, both inner and outer—

> Mist clogs the sunshine.
> Smoky dwarf houses
> Hem me round everywhere;
> A vague dejection
> Weighs down my soul—

Arnold goes on to paint a series of tiny pieces, 'prospects and beings': the gilt terraces of Lassa, the gathering of the Muses, a blind beggar, once a bold robber, in an African town, two young lovers (*must* they be Matthew and Marguerite?) wishing time might prolong their happiness. Here the poet falls a-moralising: to eternalise a happy moment for one would be to extend the misery of others, to annihilate the poet's own depression would cancel someone else's

joy (what made Arnold suppose this?) Nevertheless the poem ends
in acceptance—

> Time, so complained of,
> Who to no one man
> Shows partiality,
> Brings round to all men
> Some undimmed hours.

This, though smacking of meiosis, is wise and neatly put, and there is
no doubt that the complete freedom of such measures suited Arnold's
lesser talent. It looks easy, but is probably not as easy as it looks.

The Youth of Nature and *The Youth of Man* are two halves of one
poem, and should be read consecutively. Together they form
Arnold's greatest nature poem (the Oxford poems always excepted),
the poem in which he shows most clearly his discipleship to Wordsworth. The laureate had just died, and the *Prelude* had just been
published, but this latter event (the more important of the two)
did not, as we have seen, make any very deep impression on Arnold's
mind. But the master's death was still fresh to him, and though he
had already given perfect expression to his feelings and thoughts in
the *Memorial Verses*, he now continues his lament, not in the same
metre but in that of *Rugby Chapel*, which left him liberty of dis-
quisition but rendered unlikely another finished work of art.

The poem opens with a burst of pure lyric:

> Raised are the dripping oars,
> Silent the boat! the lake,
> Lovely and soft as a dream,
> Swims in the sheen of the moon.
> The mountains stand at its head
> Clear in the pure June night,
> But the valleys are flooded with haze.
> Rydal and Fairfield are there;
> In the shadow Wordsworth lies dead.
> So it is, so it will be for aye.
> Nature is fresh as of old,
> Is lovely; a mortal is dead.

There follows a superb use of Cumbrian proper names—

> The Pillar still broods o'er the fields
> Which border Ennerdale Lake,
> And Egremont sleeps by the sea:

not dimmed by the classical passage that succeeds.

Then he passes to Wordsworth's supreme gift: 'he was a priest to us all of the wonder and bloom of the world', and so begins an inquiry into the relation of nature and the imagination. Has the beauty of nature an objective existence, or is it imagined by the poet and 'revealed' to the rest of mankind? Are 'values' as 'real' as objects? He makes nature reply that she and her beauty are not only real but are greater than 'the poet who sings them'. 'Will ye not learn that the singer was less than his themes?' even when the theme is himself and his own emotion. Which can only mean that the language of poetry is inadequate to express and communicate the feeling that inspired it, and I do not believe this. If not poetry then music—and that blend of poetry and music which is rhythmic form. When, later in the poem, we read—

> Can the image of life have the glow,
> The motion of life itself?

one can only reply that it often seems to. Arnold goes on to elaborate his contention—or Nature's, for he makes Nature argue like a demagogue—in detail, to the end of showing that the death of a poet is not an irreparable loss while Nature herself remains. This is likely enough, but it would seem that Arnold, like Landor, put Nature first and art only second.

The poem is an inspired one. The shaky but deeply-felt argument sweeps like a great wind through the poem without pause, hesitation or lapse, finding for its expression line after line and passage after passage of beauty and power. The sequel, however, *The Youth of Man*, is much inferior; it is forced and painful, with nothing to remember except a good bit of scenic description—

> Here they stand tonight,
> Here where this grey balustrade
> Crowns the still valley. . . .

But the record of the two young people—'young, and the world is ours'—sinking through the years to a realisation of 'their faded ignoble lives', and all, apparently, because they had undervalued nature: there is nothing inspired about this or its verse. The moral of the poem is sound enough—that youth should, by 'yearning to the greatness of nature', 'rally the good in its own depths'; and the sense of something transcendent in nature is powerfully voiced in the only other memorable lines, with their echo of Wordsworth:

> Murmur of living,
> Stir of existence,
> Soul of the world!

The two poems, *A Summer Night*, published in 1852, and *A Southern Night*, 1861, are as different as two poems by the same author could be. *A Summer Night* is written, like *Dover Beach*, in free verse with rhyme, but it is no masterpiece of that form. The verse swings along with ease and power, but the form does not take possession of the thought and feeling; there is no sense of inevitability about the movement as in the greater poem. The 'far different scene' which the summer night recalls is brilliantly painted, and Arnold's favourite moonlight, with its air of tranquil assurance, sets him brooding, by contrast, on his own restless and confused mind. M. Bonnerot, who is always on the trail of Marguerite, thinks the remembered scene is one connected with that tantalising young woman, and (illogically) associates the sea-scape here described with the lake scene of the *Switzerland* poem called *Parting*. I think we must leave the scene in the obscurity of the poet's mind, and the lines about the 'unquiet breast' seem to indicate a less specialised unrest than that occasioned by Marguerite, but there is a phrase here that throws some light on the Marguerite relation. Arnold says that one of his troubles is that he is 'Never by passion quite possessed'. That is certainly the impression one gets from the

Marguerite poems, and if the phrase does properly describe Arnold's feelings there, it justifies the break with his first love: whether the case was altered in regard to his second we cannot say. He goes on to analyse (fallaciously, as I have already said) the different types of men. And then he comes to the great analogy that concludes the poem. Arnold's ideal life of the mind is figured in the cloudless night heaven—

> Plainness and clearness without shadow of stain!
> Clearness divine!

He is not content to accept the simile as such, but must go on to endow the heavens with human qualities, those he desires in himself, but presently returns to the legitimate analogy: he wishes that man, contemplating the boundless horizon of the clear sky, might catch thence a realisation of the possibilities of his own life, and of

> How fair a lot to fill
> Is left to each man still.

A poem with a lovely opening and a sublime conclusion, a little spoilt by an unnecessarily embittered middle.

A Southern Night is written in regular stanza form, and moreover in one of Arnold's most successful short stanzas. The iambic metre is handled with considerable freedom, and for once he adopts that unexpected short last line which more brilliant metrists have found effective. These features, together with an uncharacteristic amount of alliteration, are seen in the opening stanza:

> The sandy spits, the shore-locked lakes,
> Melt into open, moonlit sea;
> The soft Mediterranean breaks
> At my feet, free.

As in the other poem, the moonlit night reminds him of another night, but this time there is no doubt as to the scene in question, for a note tells us that it is the 'deserted, moon-blanched street' of *A Summer Night*. But now his unrest is forgotten, swallowed up in

memories of his dead brother, William. He feels it is wrong that
William and his wife should be buried away from their own
country, because 'we English', who 'never once possess our souls',
ought to lie amid the traffic of cities. He contrasts us with contem-
platives like Indian sages and mediaeval romantics, and then remembers that these two who are dead were so gentle and good
that they, as much as those others, were allied to the divine.

I think the poem and its conclusion mark a stage in Arnold's
thought. In *A Summer Night* all he could say was that man might, by
observing the serenity of (certain aspects of) nature, learn his
unrealised capabilities; now he is forced to admit that there are
already people whose personality and life show that humanity as
well as nature (and it is surely surprising that a great poet should
have been so loth to recognise it) can partake in the life of God
which is the life of the world.

The two *Obermann* poems mark, as I have shown, Arnold's passing
from agnostic determinism to a form of Christianity. He had found
in Senancourt's writings a refuge—as he said to Clough—'against
your *Zeitgeist*', but later, expressing his views chiefly in his prose
works, came to deplore the enervating depression that was the
inevitable result of accepting the *Obermann* outlook. Yet in his note
published in 1868 (after *Obermann II* had demonstrated his change of
attitude) he continued to give high praise to Senancour, because
his writings had charmed George Sand and Sainte-Beuve, two of
Arnold's idols.

The progress of the first poem is quite pedestrian, only coming to
life in passages describing the mountain scenery of the Swiss valley
where he was writing, and in the stanzas on Wordsworth and Goethe.
This is his third poetic venture into Wordsworth criticism, and here,
with inadequate consideration, he declares that Wordsworth
achieved his 'sweet calm' by averting his ken 'from half of human
fate'. It is true that Wordsworth's happy genius urged him to poetry
that uplifts rather than depresses, but to say (as others besides
Arnold have done) that he ignored the tragic side of life is to
forget *The Excursion* (the story of Margaret and many of the

Pastor's tales) and such lyrics as *The Sailor's Mother*, *The Thorn* and *Ruth*. However, Arnold's idea is that, Wordsworth and Goethe being out of reach, we should turn to *Obermann*, free ourselves of illusions, and die. Rigorously controlled by 'some unknown power', our only escape is through renunciation and withdrawal from the world so that we may live unspotted. This is surely a form of defeatism.

To read straight on from *Obermann I* to *Obermann Once More*— in the same simple and undistinguished stanza—is to move from winter into spring. In the interval of eighteen years, Arnold has become a new man, as is at once indicated by the different tone of the descriptive opening. For the awful Alpine track crawling up its rocky stair, the storm-clouds, the abandoned baths, the white mists and roaring torrents we now have a picture crowded with coloured memories and happy sights—full-foaming milk pails, a gentian-flowered pass, 'orchard and croft and full-stored grange', sun-warmed firs and the wild bee's hum. (What a charming fondness Arnold has for this delectable sound: we have it again in *Obermann I*; it is the sole sign of life amid the silence longed for by the lover in *Parting*; and in *Haworth Churchyard* the drowsy bee hums o'er the thyme.)

And now Obermann—'master of my wandering youth but left this many a year'—appears to him with a reproach for apparently (Arnold himself gives no sign of it) inclining to a new acceptance of his teaching.

> Thou fledst me when the ungenial earth,
> Man's workplace, lay in gloom.
> Returnst thou in her hour of birth,
> Of hopes and hearts in bloom?

To justify his deprecation of any such return, Obermann makes a remarkable survey of the progress of two thousand years, beginning with four or five stanzas of imaginative vision worth, as poetry, all the rest of both poems:

> In his cool hall, with haggard eyes,
>   The Roman noble lay;
> He drove abroad, in furious guise,
> Along the Appian Way.
>
> He made a feast, drank fierce and fast,
> And crowned his hair with flowers—
> No easier nor no quicker pass'd
> The impracticable hours.
>
> The brooding East with awe beheld
> Her impious younger world.
> The Roman tempest swelled and swelled,
> And on her head was hurled.
>
> The East bowed low before the blast
> In patient, deep disdain;
> She let the legions thunder past,
> And plunged in thought again.

He goes on to tell how Christ came to teach humility and died to enforce his teaching.

> Now he is dead! Far hence he lies
> In the lorn Syrian town;
> And on his grave, with shining eyes,
> The Syrian stars look down.

But the world was slow to adopt 'the way divine', and after centuries of apathy had to be awakened to fresh life by the French Revolution. Yet man still clung to the sterile past, and Obermann died in despair of any real improvement, seeking refuge in eternity. 'But thou', the spirit of Obermann continues—you, Matthew Arnold, once my disciple, yield not to despair as I did. The sun is risen . . .' the world's great order dawns' (this was doubtless a reflection of the twenty years of peace, prosperity and complacency that followed the end of the Crimean War), a new-made world needs the message of hope—

> One common wave of thought and joy
> Lifting mankind again.

And Arnold awakes from his dream to find the sun risen indeed:

> And glorious there without a sound,
> Across the glimmering lake,
> High in the Valais-depth profound,
> I saw the morning break.

Thus beautifully closes what is the most indisputably optimistic of Arnold's poems. The optimism expressed in the sentence, 'the world's great order dawns' proved to be unwarranted, but Arnold (or Obermann) was going on the signs of the times, and could hardly be expected to foresee the cataclysmic setback of two World Wars. The 'perplexed' generation of today, which is said to find Arnold's 'austere poetry' specially 'adapted to its spiritual needs', tends to overlook the implications of *Obermann Once More*.

The delightful love-scene that sets the stage for *The Buried Life* has a quiet tenderness which to me suggests home-life with Fanny Lucy rather than swift and sorry meetings in Swiss hotels. And there are three lines in the first paragraph—

> Give me thy hand, and hush awhile,
> And turn those limpid eyes on mine,
> And let me read there, love, thy inmost soul—

which, compared with the three lines from the *Ode on Melancholy* which perhaps suggested them—

> Or if thy mistress some rich anger shows,
> Emprison her soft hand, and let her rave,
> And feed deep, deep upon her peerless eyes—

provide some measure of the plainer diction and healthier emotion of the Victorian poet.

From this picturesque starting-point Arnold goes on to enunciate his famous distinction of man's frivolous behaviour (an only too accurate description in view of the issues involved) and the 'buried stream', the 'indiscernible flow', of his real life. This might be the 'unconscious' of modern psychology, especially when he speaks of 'airs and floating echoes' that come 'from the soul's subterranean depths'. But I think he intends these depths not only to have nothing sinister about them (an indispensable attribute of the Freudian unconscious) but to be in the last resort accessible. When he reaches his climax, the rarely occurring moment when, inspired by love, the man is able to release the powers hidden in these 'subterranean depths' and gain a knowledge of his true life, its origin, its nature, its destiny—this is more akin to the mystic experience which is born not in the unconscious mind but in the supreme spirit.

There are some lines in the poem that show both Arnold's discipleship to Wordsworth and its limitations. When Arnold says,

> But often, in the world's most crowded streets,
> But often, in the din of strife,
> There rises an unspeakable desire
> After the knowledge of our buried life. . . .
> A longing to inquire
> Into the mystery of the heart which beats
> So wild, so deep in us. . . .

we at once think of the corresponding lines in *Tintern Abbey*:

> But oft, in lonely rooms, and mid the din
> Of crowded cities. . . .

But Wordsworth takes advantage of these moments of illumination to submit himself to 'sensations sweet'—in the blood, the heart and the mind—so that the 'burthen of the mystery' of the world is lightened, and

> we are laid asleep
> In body, and become a living soul,
> While with an eye made quiet by the power
> Of harmony, and the deep power of joy,
> We see into the life of things.

Arnold, on the other hand, is spurred on to 'delve into his own breast', 'to speak and act our hidden self': what he finds and hears he feels to be untrue; he is stupefied and benumbed and made melancholy. To some extent it is simply a case of the greater genius against the less, but it is also the difference between passive submission to the inflow of light and impatient effort and questioning. Nevertheless, by the loveliness and complete adequacy of its form, and by its satisfying conclusion, *The Buried Life* is to be put amongst the greatest poems of its author.

This cannot be said of *Stanzas from the Grande Chartreuse*, though it contains two of Arnold's most pregnant lines—

> Wandering between two worlds, one dead,
> The other powerless to be born.

They seem to describe his religious position in 1855, when the poem was published in *Frazer's Magazine*. The 'dead' world is that of the Christian faith, dead to him since his youth, and—in spite of Victorian church-going—dead, he felt, for England, where, however, the prevailing mood of painful doubt perhaps kept religion alive (Blougram thought it did—'the more of doubt the more of faith, I say!'). The 'other' is the truer faith that must take its place but is still delayed. Within the next ten years Arnold had found a home of sorts in a modified, even eviscerated, Christianity—had escaped from the wistful hesitancy of the poem to the more positive condition of *Literature and Dogma*.

The poem begins with a journey to the monastery and an inaccurate but deeply felt description of a service of the monks that he was allowed to watch. He feels that he is out of place, yet that he shares with the monks the world's mockery, though, as he admits, it is his melancholy not his scepticism that is condemned. There is some bad writing here.

> Ah, if it *be* passed, take away . . .

is a shocking line; 'it' in that line is ambiguous, indicating either the old faith or his melancholy; a few lines on he says,

> But if you cannot give us ease. . . .

and we do not know who 'you' is or who are comprehended under 'us'—till now the word has been 'me'. Nor is it clear in the next stanza who are 'the kings of modern thought' who are 'dumb'.

With more force he declares that the scorn of Byron, the 'lovely wail' of Shelley, the 'sad stern page' of Obermann have left the world unredeemed. We can do nothing but wait in tears for an age

> Which without harshness will be sage
> And gay without frivolity

(this hardly amounts to a new religion, but perhaps indicates a valuable combination of tolerant wisdom and happiness). He says we—meaning himself—cannot fully accept the outlook of the times, which he exposes as materialistic and scientific, and concludes the poem with a long analogy of children living near an old-world abbey. Tinker and Lowry suggest that these last half-dozen stanzas are illogically adduced, as they seem to apply to the Carthusians, but I don't think this is a correct reading. The antithesis is not between the monks and the outside world but between the serious inquirers after truth, like Arnold, and the glib prophets of new agnostic philosophies, figured in the analogy by passing soldiers and hunters. Arnold and his kind belong to a people who have lived for too long in the atmosphere of the Church—like the children dwelling under the abbey walls—to be able to throw off its influence except at the call of something greater. They may live in a desert, but they would have their desert left in peace.

The intellectual position is unusually confused, and it would seem that the experience of finding himself amid the fervours of the devoted order disturbed the mental equilibrium of the over-rational poet.

(e) *Three Narrative Poems*

Arnold's genius was for self-expression, and did not lean either to narrative, as with Tennyson and Browning, or to Browning's instinct for dramatisation. Apart from the two classical dramas and three or four short pieces, of which *The Forsaken Merman* is not so much a story as a lyrical situation, Arnold's narrative poetry consists of three works, *Sohrab and Rustum*, *Balder Dead* and *Tristram and*

Iseult, which together amount in bulk to one of the twelve books of *The Ring and the Book* or to a couple of *Idylls.* Nevertheless, the first and last of these three poems are amongst the most striking of Arnold's achievements.

I really do not know what imp of criticism possessed Mr Eliot to make him say Landor's *Gebir* was 'a finer piece than *Sohrab and Rustum*'. It may be true that Landor, aiming more meticulously at a 'compendious and exclusive' style, can beat Arnold in that domain whenever he chooses, but surely Arnold's own insistence (in the *Preface*) on subject must be allowed some weight. Nothing less 'classical' can be imagined than the fatuous story of *Gebir,* while in the disaster through ignorance followed by recognition, which provides the motive of the story of *Sohrab and Rustum,* there is something genuinely Greek, and the firm design and severity of treatment are in the classical tradition. One may not have much use for stories of single combat between barbaric heroes, and may much prefer the kind found in *Michael, Dora* or *The Statue and the Bust,* but this one is told movingly, with masses of local colour (Arnold's knowledge of Persian history and myth was sufficient to make this convincing without descending to deadening accuracy) and imaginative detail, much of it in those extended similes already mentioned, which Arnold said he had taken great care to 'orientalise'.

> For very young he seemed, tenderly reared;
> Like some young cypress, tall and dark and straight,
> Which in a queen's secluded garden throws
> Its slight dark shadow on the moonlit turf
> By midnight, to a bubbling fountain's sound—
> So slender Sohrab seemed, so softly reared.

The blank verse goes nobly forward like a Spanish galleon before the wind, carrying the combat and its origins, with a distant glimpse of 'that sad mother' who had let Rustum think his new-born child was a girl—

> for fear
> Rustum should take the boy to train in arms—

thus contributing her thread of confusion to the tragedy. The two
heroic figures, father and son, are well-realised, and Mr Kingsmill
characteristically sees in them Thomas and Matthew. One reads, as
Arnold said he had composed, with pleasure, even if some of the
pleasure lies in the knowledge that after all the dusty conflict one is
to come to that wonderful close, the perfect realisation of calm and
vision of eternity, when that

> luminous home of waters opens bright
> And tranquil, from whose floor the new-bathed stars
> Emerge and shine upon the Aral sea.

The majestic river is anthropomorphised—

> Oxus, forgetting the bright speed he had—

but only to a degree that intensifies the sense of calm by making it
conscious. The passage brings to mind the lovely quiet close of
Paradise Lost, and it is the climax of Arnold's use of rivers, of clear
moving water.

Balder Dead is not a popular poem, and has few elements of greatness. Whether you read it at all depends on your feeling about the
Norse mythology, which (with its humour and magic—seen
combined in the insubstantial chain that bound Fenris the wolf)
I happen to enjoy better than the Greek, but I still find Arnold's
poem not exhilarating. The verse is lifeless, perhaps because so many
of the lines begin with the word 'and'. The story is clearly if heavily
told, concentrating on the pathos at the expense of the beauty and
splendour. As Arnold indicates by his note giving the antecedents
of the chosen episode, he took his version from the *Edda*, thus
avoiding Saxo's sordid version which makes Balder die in a fight
with his brother over Nanna. The story found in the *Edda* is a noble
story, though the guilelessness of the Gods and their helplessness
before the cunning of Lok are pitiful. Arnold's personal contribution
comes in the form of a comment made by Balder to his brother
Hermod, who is about to return to Heaven. Balder tells Hermod
he is not unwilling to remain in Hela's realm, because he is 'long

since weary of your storm of carnage'; he will there 'attend the course of ages' and hope to 'return to light' in a happier day. And to Hermod asking what he means Balder prophesies the emergence of 'another Heaven', a 'second Asgard', 'an earth more fresh, more verdant', where man shall live in peace while the Gods rejoice in pastime and wise discourse. This is, as a matter of fact, a transference to Balder of the vision Odin had after the sybil had told him about Ragnarok.

Were it not for certain imperfections of form, *Tristram and Iseult* would stand proudly with the other masterpieces. *Thyrsis* and *The Scholar-Gipsy*, *Dover Beach* and *The Future* are all fashioned with the art of a Phidias, conveying the poetic vision lightly and lucidly. There is an infinity of beauty in *Tristram and Iseult*, but it is overlaid, unpruned, and the poem cannot commend itself to everybody as it does to me.

Let me begin by disposing of the idea—confidently announced by M. Bonnerot and accepted by Garrod and others—that Tristram stands for Matthew Arnold, Iseult of Ireland for Marguerite, and Iseult of Brittany for Fanny Lucy. You may read these parallels into the story if you will, but you will get no support from Arnold. M. Bonnerot admits that his interpretation stands only '*dans le plan de l'imagination*', but he must believe that Arnold had the twin situations in mind as he wrote. If so, as Browning would say, the less Arnold he! *Tristram and Iseult* was published, with the Marguerite poems, in 1852, and must have been written much at the same time, at the time also when he was falling in love with Miss Wightman and marrying her. Would there not have been a certain treason in the comparisons that are set up, if they are to apply to Marguerite and Fanny Lucy? M. Bonnerot quotes the passage,

> There were two Iseults who did sway
> Each her hour of Tristram's day;
> But one possessed his waning time,
> The other his resplendent prime . . .
> She is here who had his gloom,
> Where art thou who hads't his bloom?

Is it conceivable that Arnold, who was proud of being 'literal and sincere', would write like that with his newly married wife in mind? A romantic argument, not a logical one, I am well aware. But surely there is logic in my pointing out that though the contrasting terms, 'resplendent prime' and 'waning time', 'bloom' and 'gloom', apply with great strictness to Tristram, they have no meaning when applied to Arnold, for whom the second 'Iseult' came within a year of the first. I give M. Bonnerot credit for not pressing a number of other '*rapprochements*' he sees; I will only add that I see dissimilarities too numerous to mention.

So to our story. The Tristram legend is, next to that of Helen of Troy, the most famous of all love-stories. It is unusual in that its shape is not triangular but rhombic; there are in fact two triangles sharing a common side—

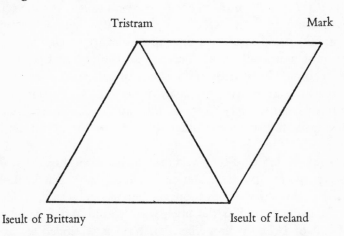

Tristram   Mark

Iseult of Brittany   Iseult of Ireland

We are accustomed to think of Tristram as one of Arthur's knights, but the story seems to have arisen independently, as a Cornish or Breton romance of the thirteenth century, associated with the name of either Thomas of Brittany or our own Thomas the Rymer, and to have been woven later into the Arthurian cycle. It has two alternative endings. In one, used by Malory (though indicated by him very briefly and inadequately), Tristram is treacherously slain by

H

Mark. This is the ending adopted by Tennyson in *The Last Tourna-
ment*, and by him given a powerful ironic twist. Tristram, having
returned from Brittany to Cornwall, is conversing with Iseult in her
bower, and she has been complaining of the traps her husband sets
to catch her. 'Mark's way!' she says. But the King is hiding close by
and presently seizes his opportunity: as Tristram is about to kiss
Iseult—

> Behind him rose a shadow and a shriek—
> 'Mark's way', said Mark, and clove him through the brain.

But one MS. gives the more romantic ending of the black and
white sails, supposed to have been suggested by the incident in the
life of Theseus. According to this, Tristram is lying in the castle on
the Breton coast, wounded to death and nursed by his wife, Iseult
of Brittany. He sends a messenger to Cornwall to implore the other
Iseult to come to him before he dies, and—desiring 'advance
information'—he tells the messenger that as he approaches the quay
he is to hoist white sails if the Queen is with him, black if she has
refused to come. His wife knows of the arrangement and sits by the
window watching: she sees the boat, its sails are white, but in her
jealous resentment she tells Tristram they are black, whereupon he
dies in despair, and when the other Iseult enters she dies upon his
body.

This is the ending used by Swinburne in his version of the story,
Tristram of Lyonesse (which I confess I cannot read). But Wagner,
remodelling the story for his opera, *Tristan and Isolde*, written
within the same period as the poems of Arnold and Swinburne,
omits Iseult of Brittany altogether. Tristram is wounded to death
by one of Mark's knights, and he and Isolde of Cornwall die
together to the music of the Liebestod.

Now there are several interesting things about Arnold's handling
of the story, which he said he read not only in Malory but in an
article in a French journal that he came across in Thun (this last fact
is thought to strengthen the case for the personal parallel). This
French version contained the black and white sails ending, but

Arnold did not use it, though he made Tristram die in the Breton castle, nursed by Iseult of Brittany, and send the messenger for Iseult of Ireland. I imagine he omitted the incident of the sails because it involved Iseult's false announcement, and he could not bear to attribute jealousy and deception to 'the sweetest Christian soul alive'. This was not just chivalry. Arnold had evidently fallen in love with the princess of the white hands, and he treats her tenderly throughout. In the old legends it is made clear that her marriage with Tristram was a 'marriage only in name', and Swinburne (than whom it is impossible to conceive a greater contrast with Arnold in every respect) is profuse in his sneers at the 'married maiden', 'virgin wife'. Arnold boldly gives her two children, and devotes a whole Part III to her after Tristram and the haughtier Iseult are dead.

Structurally, Arnold's handling of the great story is more original than we might have expected. He not so much plunges *in medias res* as comes in at the death. The poem covers only the last few hours of Tristram's long and adventurous life, earlier incidents—just in so far as they are relevant—being told in a series of what we now call flash-backs. Three times is the magical episode of the love-potion told: first as a piece of plain narrative in the setting of the characters—

> That proud, first Iseult, Cornwall's queen—
> She whom Tristram's ship of yore
> From Ireland to Cornwall bore . . .
> She who as they voyaged quaffed
> With Tristram that spiced magic draught
> Which since then for ever rolls
> Through their blood and binds their souls . . .

then as a memory, muttered by Tristram in his sleep, of Iseult's words in the ship—

> 'Tristram, I pray thee, of thy courtesy
> Reach me my golden cup that stands by thee,
> But pledge me in it first for courtesy.'
> Ha! dost thou start? are thy lips blanched like mine?
> Child, 'tis no true draught this, 'tis poisoned wine!

and again as a narrative of his dream—

> Ah, sweet angels, let him dream . . .
> Let them drink it—let their hands
> Tremble and their cheeks be flame,
> As they feel the fatal bands
> Of a love they dare not name
> With a wild delicious pain
> Twine about their hearts . . .

Besides this source of all the sorrow and all the romance, the narrative gives us sharp vignettes of the three figures—

> The peerless hunter, harper, knight,
> Tristram of Lyonesse;

the 'snowdrop by the sea'—

> I know her by her mildness rare,
> Her snow-white hands, her golden hair . . .
> And her fragile loveliness—
> The sweetest Christian soul alive,
> Iseult of Brittany;

and the other Iseult, with

> her proud dark eyes
> And her petulant quick replies,
> . . . her dazzling hand . . . her raven hair.

Apart from the narrative, it is through Tristram's racing thoughts under his closed eyelids that we get glimpses of most of the adventurous story—the secret and dangerous meetings of the star-crossed lovers; Tristram's banishment and finding of the 'lovely orphan child' in her castle by the coast, presently 'his timid youthful bride'; his wars and wanderings, the first Iseult always in his brain—

> Above the din her voice is in my ears,
> I see her form glide through the crossing spears.
> Iseult!

Then Tristram, waking, turns to his wife and speaks of his children. And the narrative gives a long and intimate, emotional, perhaps sentimental picture (Arnold had just become a father) of the two children asleep and dreaming.

All this narrative is composed in a metre that often recalls *Christabel*. The metrical structure of the poem is interesting. In this first part, all the Tristram passages, whether speech or dream, are written in a powerful movement of dramatic rhymed pentameters, and the interspersed narrative in octosyllables, with the variations that recall *Christabel*—

> What knight is this, so weak and pale,
> Though the locks are yet brown on his noble head? . . .
>
> Loud howls the wind, sharp patters the rain,
> And the knight sinks back on his pillows again.

Tristram's pentameters, and especially those parts of his dream that end with the agonised cry, 'Iseult!', convey the authentic passion of the magic draught, and the narrative moves on quicker feet to keep the spell unbroken. Then at the end of Part I, after a long passage of tetrameters, during which we almost forget the tension of the waiting, suddenly there breaks in a single anapaestic couplet—

> What voices are these on the clear night air?
> What lights in the court? what steps on the stair?

and we are in Part II, called *Iseult of Ireland*.

Arnold said he was dissatisfied with this part—he thought it 'monotonous'. That does not seem to be its weakness, but rather artificiality due to the stanza-form chosen for the dialogue of Tristram and the Iseult who has come at his call. For this, Arnold changed to trochaic pentameters in quatrains, rhyming *a b c b*. Elsewhere, in shorter measures, he is successful enough with the trochee, but here the effect is simply stilted, which is a pity, as these two have much to express. What a scene it would have made in blank verse; I suppose Arnold was afraid of it and clamped down on passion with this lolloping metre.

It does not seem right, either, that Tristram should begin by reproaching Iseult bitterly for her delay. However, the lovers are presently talking pathetically, till Tristram falls back in his death throe, commending Iseult to make friends with his wife and live with her—a proposition which M. Bonnerot fitly describes as '*plus émouvante que vraisemblable*'. Instead, Iseult dies with Tristram. Their last words are worth quoting, if only to show how much better Arnold's second thoughts could be than his first:

> *Tristram.*   Now to sail the sea of death I leave thee.
>   One last kiss upon the living shore!
> *Iseult.*   Tristram! Tristram!—stay—receive me with thee!
>   Iseult leaves thee, Tristram, never more.

Tinker and Lowry's note tells us that these lines appeared in a different form in 1852, ending (unbelievably),

> Ah Sorrow—
> Fool! thou missest—we are both unmoved!

Here the legend ends, but Arnold has still much to say. He lavishes some of his richest and most moving description on Iseult as she lies in the moonlight, dead by her dead lover. The passion which, day and night, had 'consumed her beauty like a flower', is overpast, and in her face a freshness as of her prime returns to express 'a tranquil, settled loveliness'. Part of this description (II, 131-146) originally belonged to the poem called *Youth and Calm* (first called *Lines by a Death-bed*) and was afterwards (not till 1869) transplanted to *Tristram*. The appropriateness of the lines for their new situation (including the final line, 'Her younger rival's purest grace') is astonishing. The fact of the transference seems to me odd, but the passage shows that Arnold's kindly feeling was not confined to Iseult of Brittany.[1]

There follows a passage surprisingly reminiscent of Keats, where

---

[1] There is some nice work to be done here by the upholders of the theory that the two Iseults are Marguerite and Fanny Lucy, but I am not disposed to do it for them.

Arnold tells how the night-air 'flaps the ghostlike tapestry' in the chamber 'where those lifeless lovers lie', and how a Huntsman in the arras looks down on them. As *The Eve of St Agnes* ends

> Ay, ages long ago
> These lovers fled away into the storm,

so here

> these thou seest are unmoved,
> Cold, cold as those who lived and loved
> A thousand years ago.

And there is still Arnold's own contribution, Part III, *Iseult of Brittany*, where for once he adopted Browning's regular habit of giving a new ending to a tale he was retelling. This third part is short, but should have been shorter. The two moralising paragraphs about 'the gradual furnace of the world' and 'this fool passion' are entirely supererogatory, and it would have been artistically good to omit the two preceding paragraphs also—to go straight on from the point where Iseult led the children home to that which asks

> What tale did Iseult to the children say
> Under the hollies that bright winter's day?

But Arnold wanted those two paragraphs for the opportunity they afforded him to give further voice to the love he has conceived for 'the young surviving Iseult', whom joy has not yet found, nor ever will. So he talks on about her with a beautiful tenderness before he comes to the tale she told her children, the tale of Merlin and Vivian, which had attracted him when he came on it in Malory. It is interesting to compare the three versions, Malory's, Tennyson's and Arnold's. Malory's is a brief plain narrative, chiefly notable for the pathos of Merlin's reply to Arthur, 'Nay, it will not be', when the King has asked him why, if he knew the danger he was in from Vivian's (Nimue's) wiles, he did not 'purvey for it'—'No, I am helpless, I can do nothing about it.' Tennyson let the bitter little tale sink into his imagination, where it swelled and burgeoned into

the great Idyll, the protracted deadly struggle between aged cunning
and youthful wickedness, pivoted on the terrible epigram,

> For men at most differ as Heaven and earth,
> But women, worst and best, as Heaven and Hell.

Arnold's version is again short, and not only short but sweet, as
befits a tale, 'an old world Breton history', told by a gentle mother
to her children. All the poison that seeps out of the Idyll is removed.
It is Vivian's beauty not her badness that is dwelt upon, the brown
locks of her hair playing on her flushed cheek and her blue eyes
sparkling—

> Her 'haviour had the morning's fresh clear grace,
> The spirit of the woods was in her face.

Her wickedness is barely and casually hinted at, as Merlin comes
through the forest glades of Broceliande with 'that false fay, his
friend'. Nor is there any struggle or fear—just that Merlin's 'best
wits took flight as he grew fond'. And when they are sitting among
the primroses Merlin falls asleep, and Vivian, finger on lip, rises,
waves her wimple nine times round, 'and made a little plot of magic
ground' to imprison Merlin till the judgement day. And all because
—very naturally—'she was passing weary of his love'. Arnold took
the phrase from Malory, but placed it artistically at the end of the
story, which is told in beautiful lyrical couplets that stand up well
to Tennyson's strong dramatic blank verse. Put the dialogue in Part II
into something more expressive than trochaics, and cut Part III a
little, and *Tristram and Iseult* would be a very great poem—as indeed
it is, and also a poem of lasting delight.

(f) *Five Lyric Poems*

The Forsaken Merman is placed among the narrative poems, but
is as essentially lyrical as *La Belle Dame Sans Merci*. It has the two
elements of lyric, singing quality and intense personal feeling.
For the second, I do not believe it includes much of the Marguerite

motif. Doubtless Arnold took some pleasure in substituting the name Margaret for the ones he found in the various versions of the Danish folk-ballad, but the situations are too widely different to be made to run parallel, and if he meant the plaint, 'There dwells a loved one but cruel is she', to apply to Marguerite he was being unfair.

Of the three 'personages' of the poem, the Merman, Margaret and the sea, the third is the most interesting, and one could not have expected that Arnold, so familiar with Westmorland lake and river and Oxford countryside, would be so excellent an interpreter of the spirit of ocean's kingdom. Only in this poem does he display this special power. In the poem *To a Gipsy-child by the Sea-shore* both sea and shore are forgotten, and the grating roar of the receding waves on Dover Beach is the sound heard by a landsman. But the watery home of the Merman is painted for us with the intimacy of a lover and the hand of an artist, from the great winds, the salt tides and the white horses of the first paragraph to the sand-strewn caverns, cool and deep, with all their accompaniments of sea-snakes and great whales sailing with unshut eye, all most exquisitely realised, to the ceiling of amber and pavement of pearl of the Merman's retreat from sorrow. As with *Tristram and Iseult*, we begin at the end of the story and are told later, with nicest artistic propriety, of the story that led up to that end. No praise could be too high for the artistry of the narrative and the parallel development of the Merman's feelings. Exception has been taken to the irregular metrical form, but the tightest hand is kept on the varying line-length, so that (as in *The Future* and *Dover Beach*) we feel all the force that normally belongs to regular metre. As a matter of fact, most of the poem is in regular couplets, of two or four feet (iambics mixed with anapaests), and the whole makes a music rich and strange that lingers unforgettably on the ear. Saintsbury calls the poem poetically beautiful and prosodically excellent. (This is in the *History of Prosody*: the puzzling adverse criticism which I noted in an earlier chapter is from the monograph.)

Philomela has the brevity of an anguished cry. Arnold has accepted

the legend and read, through the melancholy of his own temperament, the nightingale's song as the expression of inextinguishable
grief. He takes the opportunity to depict, as a salve for the wounds,
some of his own best-loved nature-pieces—the

> fragrant lawn
> With its cool trees, and night,
> And the sweet, tranquil Thames,
> And moonshine, and the dew . . .
> . . . the moonlight on the English grass.

It is unnecessary to point out (especially as Coleridge did it so well
in his 'conversation piece') that the nightingale's song voices grief
only to those whose ears are tuned to grief. As Keats sat in the
Hampstead garden—his state of mind not over-hopeful—he heard
the nightingale singing of summer in full-throated ease, and was
made happy in its happiness, though I am not suggesting that it is
this more cheerful sensitivity that makes the *Ode* an even greater
poem than Arnold's perfect if comparatively shapeless lyric. Tinker
and Lowry's notes show some terribly inferior stuff that was
afterwards rejected, and there is that inspired epithet, 'tawny-
throated', which only came after 'inken-throated' had been tried.
These two variants have caused critics some pain. Far from thinking
'tawny-throated' inspired, Garrod said it must be a mistake for
'tawny-billed', and Middleton Murry,[1] while accepting 'tawny-
throated', found it difficult to believe that Arnold actually wrote
'inken-throated' at any time. These two eminent and admirable
critics are obviously taking 'tawny' and 'inken' as applying to the
bird's feathery colour. To me it seems clear that they have a different
kind of reference. 'Inken-throated' means singing in the dark ('the
wakeful bird sings darkling' was doubtless better) and 'tawny-
throated' means singing with passion. (Surely 'tawny' suggests
fierceness, passion?)

   The last lines,

> Eternal passion!
> Eternal pain!

[1] 'Matthew Arnold Today', *The Times Literary Supplement*, April 6, 1946.

are less profound in meaning than the lines of Browning they recall—

> Infinite passion and the pain
> Of finite hearts that yearn.

Arnold's words mean only that passion is always accompanied by pain, so that if passion is eternal pain is eternal too; Browning suggests more fruitfully that with some of us, at least, the heart is an inadequate vehicle for that movement of the spirit, that more than human condition, we call passion, so that the attempt of the lesser to carry the greater is likely to bring pain. But given the point of view, the resultant feeling and interpretation of the nightingale's song could not be more poignantly, lyrically, beautifully rendered.

Bacchanalia: or the New Age has an intellectual rather than a poetical interest. Saintsbury saw humour in it, but even if satire always has an element of humour, I don't think Arnold intended any very pointed humour here.[1] The poem is in two halves, designed as parallel but not in fact quite so. The noisy irruption in the second part is different in kind and especially in effect from that of the first. We lead off with the only really beautiful part of the poem, an utterly lovely description (with echoes of *L'Allegro* and the *Elegy*) of a quiet evening in the country. The quiet is rudely broken by a crowd of dancing and singing Maenads. They are emblems of joy and beauty, but the shepherd says (or implies) that the silence they have shattered was more beautiful still. Then, as a parallel to the evening scene, we have a critical appreciation of an age just past— doubtless Arnold had in mind the first and greater Romantic period, ending about 1830. This again is shown as broken in upon by the new age with its crowding geniuses of 'art, science, wit'. But one age does not break in upon another like this, because 'ages' do not begin suddenly and end sharply. What Arnold means is that there is a restfulness in looking back over a bygone period, known, loved and accepted (like the feeling of security in taking up for the

---

[1] Arnold, waggish in conversation, became very serious as soon as he sat down to write verse. The only places where I find him funny are in those occasional lines which, read in isolation, convey an unintended sense, as, 'When I shall be divorced some ten years hence', or 'tears are in his eyes and in his ears'.

twentieth time *Esmond* or *The Prelude*), and little but bewilderment
and confusion in trying to assess the multitudinous new 'works' of
one's own time. They have brilliance, and some of them must have
value, but the light of the new day is garish, and if we allow ourselves
to be absorbed in it we may lose the capability of enjoying the
voices that speak out of the diviner silence of the past. Arnold is a
little unkind in arrogating only to the poet the power to 'feel the
past as well'.

If Arnold were indeed objecting to 'the new age' bursting in
torrents over the still world of the past epoch, it is worth noting
that the works just being published as he wrote were not of a very
objectionable kind, including as they did *Alice in Wonderland*,
Sesame and Lilies, early novels of 'Ouida' and Meredith and late ones
by Dickens, together with his own first series of *Essays in Criticism*.
He may have found Swinburne's *Poems and Ballads* and Newman's
Apologia more disturbing.

The *Lines Written in Kensington Gardens* show Arnold's realisation
of a thing that is ignored by some who fret about the spread of
civilisation and exaggerate the extent of its destruction of natural
beauty, ignoring also the special and unique beauty that results from
the co-operation of man with nature. This is charmingly shown
in the third stanza:

> Sometimes a child will cross the glade
> To take his nurse his broken toy;
> Sometimes a thrush flit overhead
> Deep in her unknown day's employ.

In Arnold's day this special beauty could be found in London
itself; now perhaps one must go a little way out, say as far as the
Mickleham Downs. Arnold declares that in his cradle he 'was
breathed on by the rural Pan', but the passion thus inspired does not
demand unvisited and untamed nature all the time. The 'endless,
active life' in the grass and trees of the Gardens is almost as wonderful
as that known by the angler by a lonely mountain stream. In this
green and not too secluded place he finds peace and solace against

'the impious uproar' of the world, and he calls upon the 'calm soul of all things' to make it always possible for him to feel, wherever he may be, the indestructible life of nature, whence he may learn the stoic strength and self-sufficiency.

Urania is a beautiful and interesting poem. It is generally read as a 'Marguerite' poem, and its original title, *Excuse*, suggests that it might have been written to excuse that young woman's wayward-ness. Buxton Forman, editing the poem in the Temple Classics series, sub-titled it 'The Muse's Scorn': this is poetic but unconvinc-ing, and Arnold probably intended by the new title not the Muse but the Goddess. But I don't believe he was writing about either Marguerite (though she will have 'touched him off') or a muse or a goddess, or even about himself. The poem opens with the pronoun 'I', but for the rest it employs the plural number—'we', 'our', 'men'; it is not about himself and Marguerite but about man and woman. Marguerite's 'mocking' behaviour is nowhere else referred to as 'cold', or even 'light', and I believe that when Arnold writes,

> She is not cold, she is not light,
> But our ignoble souls lack might,

he is speaking of woman *vis-à-vis* man. The first words of the poem, 'I too have suffered', suggest that something, some reference to others, has gone before, or is implied. Let us suppose that Arnold had written, or thought, or come upon, some such twisted version of Scott as this:

> O woman, to the anguished brow
> A ministering angel thou,
> Yet in our fleeting hour of ease,
> How cold, how light, how hard to please!

Yes, says Arnold, thinking first of Marguerite and then accepting the generalisation, Yes—

> I too have suffered; yet I know
> She is not cold, though she seems so;
> She is not cold, she is not light;
> But our ignoble souls lack might.

And he goes on to develop this theme—man and his deficiencies,

> Our petty souls, our strutting wits,
> Our laboured, puny passion fits—

till he comes to the conception of a truly right companion for woman, some greater man, 'one of some worthier race than ours':

> His eyes be like the starry lights,
> His voice like sounds of summer nights;
> In all his lovely mien let pierce
> The magic of the universe!

Surely all this is rather ridiculously over-drawn if it is to be considered simply as the finding of someone worthy of Marguerite,[1] but imaginatively true as matching up to a high ideal of womanhood. It is true that Arnold does not elsewhere (except perhaps in the figure of Merope) offer much evidence of even this degree of feminism—which is I think justified by the probability that most men are unworthy of most women, at least are incapable of returning an equal love. The whole double sequence of love-poems is written entirely from the man's point of view, and may be contrasted with the sequence called *James Lee's Wife* of that more genuine feminist, Robert Browning.

Urania seems to return to Marguerite in the exquisite final couplet—

> Till then, her lovely eyes maintain
> Their pure, unwavering, deep disdain—

which however is no less applicable to woman herself as conceived throughout the poem, and is a little too serious for the quality attributed to Marguerite.

---

[1] Though one remembers Marchbanks' demand for an archangel as the only fit mate for Candida.

(g) *The Two Oxford Poems*

Much as he enjoyed holidays at Fox How, Arnold never acquired his father's passionate love for the Lakes, but he told his mother he could not describe the effect the Oxford landscape had on him. However, although an intimate knowledge of the Lake country doubles one's appreciation of those poems of Wordsworth that have the district for their theme or background (and indeed increases the understanding of all Wordsworth's poetry), an acquaintance with Oxfordshire and Berkshire is not necessary to a full appreciation of these two poems, though, having come to enjoy the poems for their own sake, one will naturally want to go and ascend the modest Cumnor heights and wander along the infant Isis by Wytham and Godstow and Bablock Hythe.

The stanza adopted for both poems is Arnold's single attempt, and a completely successful one, at a highly artificial and complicated verse form. His more characteristic innovations lay in the realm of 'free verse' and other loose metres, and it is astonishing that at about the same time that he was pouring out the attractive but formless fragments of *The Strayed Reveller* he was also contriving the tightest and most disciplined of all his metrical forms. That the result is excellent in both cases must increase our respect for his gifts as a craftsman. There is not much doubt that the basis of the stanza is to be found in that of the *Ode to a Nightingale*, but a very great deal has been done with it, mainly by manipulation of the rhyme-scheme. Keats begins with a quatrain rhyming *a b a b*, and follows this with a sort of sestet rhyming *c d e c d e*, of which the fourth line is shortened from five feet to three. Arnold also starts with a quatrain, but with the formula *a b c b*, and rounds this off with two lines linked with the quatrain by the rhymes *c a*, the last line, with its rhyme reaching so far back as to be almost negligible, being short like Keats's eighth line. The stanza finishes with another and very decided quatrain rhyming *d e e d*, which gives an entirely new distribution of weight within the stanza.

Keats	Arnold
a	*a*
b	*b*
a	*c*
b	*b*
c	*c*
d	*a* (short)
e	*d*
(short) *c*	*e*
d	*e*
e	*d*

The position of Arnold's short line is chosen with greater deliberation, though nothing could exceed the effect of Keats's more casual placing. The exigencies of the stanza never seem to give Arnold any difficulty, and the rhymes (as usual he chooses not to have more than two words rhyming to one sound) are handled with great charm, sometimes even (that final justification of rhyme) providing inspiration: 'all gone to rest'—'renew the quest', 'summer heats'—'shy retreats', 'Cumner range'—'sequestered grange', 'copse and briers'—'dreaming spires'.

Mr Jump says slightingly that *The Scholar-Gipsy* provides us with a pastoral week-end. And why not? Harold Monro called the train that took him to such a week-end 'the twelve o'clock to Paradise'. (But then Monro was that ill-favoured thing, a Georgian.) This week-end moreover is to be spent where 'the eye travels down to Oxford's towers'. The first three stanzas paint for us what M. Bonnerot properly calls a pre-Raphaelite picture, inexhaustibly beautiful, of the scene, by day and night, observable from the 'high field's dark corner' to which the poet's shepherd friend (not, I think, Clough) is to return that together they may renew the quest[1] for the secret of peace. Arnold was always looking for that 'citadel

---

[1] Arnold rang the changes on 'again begin the quest' and 'again renew the quest': he settled on the former, which is the better, but surely 'with me renew the quest' would have been better still.

of values' in which Charles Morgan said a man might live while
material values perish: a contemplative stillness, a quietness of
spirit, that could come through the exercise of the imagination.
Arnold seems to have thought it might have been easier to achieve
outside his own day; what he would have thought of our age of
futile speed one dare not think.

Whatever the source of the Scholar's quietism, the first half of the
poem, after the descriptive opening, presents a memorable series
of intimate pictures of the Oxford scenes through which he is
imagined as roaming, now as in his own day. No summary or
paraphrase could do anything but ruin those brilliant sketches of the
Hurst in Spring, the lone ale-house in the Berkshire moors, the boat
moored by the cool river-bank under the warm, green-muffled
Cumnor hills, the Oxford riders crossing the ferry on a summer
night, the maidens dancing round the Fyfield elm, haytime above
Godstow Bridge, the glittering river haunted by black-winged
swallows, the children ranging for cresses, the skirts of Bagley
Wood with the gipsy tents, the forest ground called Thessaly where
the blackbird fearlessly picks his food (only Chambers has been able
to identify 'Thessaly' as 'an outlier of Bagley Wood'), the wooden
bridge leading to S. Hinksey, and 'The line of festal lights in Christ
Church hall'. All is done with loving artistry, and the spirit of the
Gipsy fills all these places with an air of carefree meditative happiness.

And then we pass out of summer into autumn. To show why the
Scholar-Gipsy, like Keats's nightingale, is immortal, Arnold gives a
bitter analysis of the life he escaped by being born

> in days when wits were fresh and clear,
> And life ran gaily as the sparkling Thames.

As to that, since Glanvil's book was written in 1681, one may
suppose that the 'days' referred to belonged to that period, one in
which the persecution of the dissenters in England and brutal
hounding of the Covenanters in Scotland was beginning, so that
it is possible that life did not run gaily for everybody. And for the

I

tempo of the contrasted mid-nineteenth century, it is Arnold's own
reaction to it that is presented in such lines as

> Who fluctuate idly without term or scope . . .
> Light half-believers in our casual creeds . . .
> Whose vague resolves never have been fulfilled,

and in his diagnosis of

> this strange disease of modern life,
> With its sick hurry, its divided aims,
> Its heads o'er taxed, its palsied hearts.

He particularises one 'who most has suffered', and who

> takes dejectedly
> His seat upon the intellectual throne.

Questioned, Arnold said he meant Goethe. As Goethe had died in
1832 this was an obvious evasion, and it is quite clear that he had
Tennyson in mind. To a poet the Laureateship is naturally the
intellectual throne (though there is another which Arnold himself
was afterwards to occupy), and the rest of the stanza is a complete
portrait of the Tennyson who had recently published *In Memoriam*,
the last line, 'And all his hourly varied anodynes', being a clear
reference to

> The sad mechanic exercise
> Like dull narcotics, numbing pain.

(I suppose the line in the *Grande Chartreuse*, 'Achilles ponders in his
tent', likewise means Tennyson.)

But the true and valuable distinction drawn between the Gipsy
and the others is that he waits for 'the spark from heaven' (which
M. Bonnerot perspicaciously equates with Wordsworth's 'wise
passiveness') while Arnold and his kind wear out their lives upon a
thousand schemes. So the Gipsy is exhorted to nurse the unconquerable hope, and to this end to fly from our feverish contact as the
Tyrian trader fled the Greeks. The great and glorious simile that
ends the poem (and which for Mr Blunden brings on a new liberty,

an even wider horizon) has come in for much abuse from high authorities, but it seems all right to me. They say that the motives that prompted the trader's flight were not those which Arnold thought should urge the Scholar to 'fly our greetings, fly our speech and smiles'. But Milton's prototypes show that irrelevance of detail is one of the characteristics of the extended simile. All Arnold required was the analogy of someone getting away in a hurry from someone he does not approve of, and this he gives us in vivid colours, throwing in for good measure a piece of illustrated history. As for 'come'—'And saw the merry Grecian coaster come'— being a participle, as claimed by Messrs Tinker and Lowry, a construction more foreign to Arnold is difficult to imagine. The necessity for this uncomfortable reading is said to be that as the Grecian coaster was there already it could not be said to 'come', but you have only to read 'come out', 'emerge' (as four lines previously), and the difficulty (if there ever was one) vanishes.

Arnold fashioned three memorable tail-pieces for his greater poems—the majestic Oxus floating on, Iseult's tale of Merlin and Vivian, and this noble analogy; and if the first is easily greatest, there is little to choose between the other two. *The Scholar-Gipsy*, one of the poetic masterpieces of the century, would be a lesser thing without its finial.

Arnold complained of *The Scholar-Gipsy* that it did not 'animate'. Perhaps (after the first half) it does not, except aesthetically: all great art animates. However, *Thyrsis* atones for anything that may be missing in this way from the *Gipsy*. *Thyrsis* is the lightest-hearted of the four elegies, as *In Memoriam* is the saddest. There was every reason why, of these two elegies arising out of personal friendship, Tennyson's should betray the deeper grief. It is death in youth that rightly rouses pain and bitterness. Clough had had nearly twice Hallam's span of life. The pathos of *In Memoriam* is lacerating, that of *Thyrsis* adult and judicious. But the root of the difference lies in the approach of the two elegiasts. Tennyson brooded for ten years over the loss of his friend, letting his feelings crystallise from time to time in a jewelled lyric of memory and grief and gradually encasing them in a matrix of religious musing. Arnold waited about half that time before 'relieving himself' of his feelings, meanwhile getting on with his daily work: then he revisited the scenes associated with the Clough years, and, inspired by the beauty and the happy memories, wrote his poem, a supreme work of art and an utterly delightful tribute to the personality of his friend.

Arthur Hugh Clough was not unworthy of the tribute. He had many friends who loved him and believed in him, and if he did not quite fulfil their predictions he did many excellent things in the time that was given him. He was known as gentle and humane, with a high moral and religious sense. Arnold, in his first lecture after Clough's death, spoke of him as having no taint of littleness. His single-minded love of truth gave him great influence as a Fellow of Oriel, and his constructive ideas came forth in a flow of magical talk. But he was not only an intellectual: he had a love of life and outward things which contributes to the exhilaration of the *Bothie*. Arnold, with his passion for clear water, ought to have forgiven Clough much that he disliked in this life-abundant poem for the sake of the description of that Highland stream which came down among the heather and formed a hidden basin partly full of foam 'but mostly pellucid, pure, a mirror', where

> You are shut in, left alone with yourself and perfection of water,
> Hid on all sides, left alone with yourself and the goddess of
> bathing.
> Here the pride of the plunger, you stride the fall and clear it;
> Here the delight of the bather, you roll in beaded sparklings;
> Here into pure green depths drop down from lofty ledges.

It is this poetic and personal aspect of Clough that got into *Thyrsis*. Arnold was apologetic about having left out the philosophic, 'prophetic' side, but his instinct was sound.

The poem was supposed to be modelled on Theocritus, but apart from the names Corydon and Thyrsis there are few signs of the progenitor other than in the pastoral tone. Arnold claimed that the style was 'so artless as to be almost heedless', but this is generally wide of the mark.'Heedless' is the last word to be applied to style and diction in such a passage as—

> Humid the air; leafless, yet soft as spring,
> The tender purple spray on copse and briers!
> And that sweet city with her dreaming spires,
> She needs not June for beauty's heightening.

The poem begins with the 'refresher' visit Arnold is making to the countryside he and his friend had known of old—'Thyrsis and I: we still had Thyrsis then'. This is the first of the many expressions of controlled grief that are scattered through the poem. Soon we have the first reference to the elm-tree that had meant so much to the two young poets: 'the Signal-elm that looks on Ilsley Downs'. There are two 'trees' in these poems, and it is desirable to get them clearly distinguished. (M. Bonnerot is amused at the 'typically English' discussion of this matter.) One is 'the Fyfield tree' that Arnold in the eleventh stanza of *Thyrsis* says he 'knows', and this of course is the 'Fyfield elm' round which the maidens danced in *The Scholar-Gipsy*. It is (or was) some miles further from Oxford than the much more frequently mentioned 'signal-elm', which was on the Oxford side of Boars Hill. I say 'was' again because Sir Francis Wiley, having sought out and found the tree, discovered it to be (now) an oak.[1] In the third stanza we have the first reference to the belief cherished by Arnold and Clough that while the tree continued to stand the Scholar-Gipsy was not dead. For a time, in the poem, Arnold cannot find the tree, and wonders if it is gone; it is not till the sixteenth stanza that, in his desire to avoid a troop of hunters, he moves to another spot and finds that from there he can see the tree—'Bare on its lonely ridge, the tree, the Tree!'

Returning to the poem, we hear Arnold's lament, 'My pipe is lost, my shepherd's holiday'—he was writing less, though not less good, poetry—because he has had to 'depart into the world'—get

---

[1] But for finality on the tree, its kind, position and existence, the reader is referred to Chambers' brilliant essay, *Matthew Arnold's Tree*, in *A Sheaf of Essays*.

absorbed in the Civil Service. 'But Thyrsis of his own will went away.' Clough had thrown up his Oriel Fellowship and gone to America, 'for that a shadow loured on the fields' (I don't think it is clear what Arnold meant by this), so that his piping had taken 'a troubled sound'—not more troubled than Corydon's, one might suggest. Then comes the lovely analogy of 'the cuckoo's parting cry', heard

> some tempestuous morn in early June
> When the year's primal burst of bloom is o'er.

The critics again protest with some passion that the cuckoo does not in fact leave our shores in June, but I do not know that anyone goes so far as to suggest that Arnold should have written, 'So some tempestuous morn in early August'. Playing an unaccustomed part, Arnold reproves both Clough and the cuckoo for too readily despairing and departing. He returns to his search for the tree-topped hill with the loveliest and most intimate pictures (richer and more detailed than those in *The Scholar-Gipsy*) of spots shared with Clough —wood and slopes, dingles and hill-sides, the girl who unmoored their skiff and the mowers who stood with suspended scythe to see them pass. Night begins to fall, and he lapses into a characteristic mood of melancholy—age coming upon him, hope crushed, the way long, the fort of the world unbreachable.

Then, by fortunate accident, he finds the tree and 'takes the omen', and from this point the poem becomes a song of hope (the usual elegiac change: 'Peace, peace, he is not dead, he doth not sleep'— 'Weep no more, woeful shepherds, weep no more, For Lycidas, your sorrow, isnot dead'). 'Hear it, O Thyrsis, still our tree is there!' —and 'our Gipsy-Scholar' still haunts the fields and woods. And when Arnold begins to lament his own inability to wander like the Gipsy, he hears his friend's voice speaking words of constant encouragement:

> Why faintest thou? I wandered till I died.
> Roam on! The light we sought is shining still.
> Dost thou ask proof? Our tree yet crowns the hill,
> Our Scholar travels yet the loved hill-side.

What does it mean, in practical, non-fanciful terms? That life with and according to nature—hard but not impossible in a bustling world—is a means to that quietness of spirit for which the Gipsy-Scholar stands; perhaps even that one impulse from a vernal wood, or from one lonely tree, can be of infinite value in providing that significant awareness, that mystical apprehension of life, without which we are just Inspectors of Schools or Professors of Poetry.

It is only here that *Thyrsis* can be said to have behind it an element of religious meaning. *In Memoriam* and *Lycidas* arise clearly out of Christian belief, unquestioned by Milton, threaded through with doubt for Tennyson. *Thyrsis*, like *Adonais*, is frankly pagan. The difference does not in any way affect the artistic excellence of the four poems, but a poem on death is null and void unless it contains some implication of immortality. In *Lycidas* this is present in terms of simple Christianity—

> So Lycidas, sunk low, but mounted high
> Through the dear might of Him who walked the waves.

The after-life postulated by Tennyson is also that of the reunion taught by the Christian church—

> My Arthur, whom I shall not see
> Till all my widowed race be run.

For Shelley, Keats has gone into the white impersonal radiance of eternity—'He is made one with Nature . . .' Arnold accepts, for the purpose of the elegy, the Greek belief in the immortality of the soul enunciated by Socrates when he told Cebes and Simmias he did not grieve at death because he was 'as sure as one can be in such matters' that he was going to live with the gods. So Thyrsis is to be with Proserpine in those Italian lands where her 'rape' took place, and where Clough was buried:

> To a boon southern country he has fled,
>   And now in happier air
> Wandering with the great Mother's train divine . . .
> Within a folding of the Appenine
> Thou hearest the immortal chants of old.

But the essential immortality of Thyrsis is that of the Gipsy, the endless life of the imagination, a wandering and waiting for the spark from heaven and the vision of the Tree.

The landscape art, the nature poetry, of these two Oxford poems has received much attention. It is passionate, yet minutely faithful to truth. Swinburne called the verse of the two poems 'English coloured'. When, in an earlier chapter, I quoted some of Arnold's memorable lines I said many others could be adduced from *The Scholar-Gipsy* and *Thyrsis*. There are indeed far more than one ought to take up space with, but a few of the more famous are here printed:

Crossing the stripling Thames at Bablock-hithe.

Dark bluebells drenched with dews of summer eves.

o'er thy unknown grave
Tall grasses and white flowering nettles wave
Under a dark, red-fruited yew-tree's shade.

O born in days when wits were fresh and clear
And life ran gaily as the sparkling Thames.

And that sweet city with her dreaming spires,
She needs not June for beauty's heightening.

his piping took a troubled sound
Of storms that rage outside our happy ground;
He could not wait their passing, he is dead.

But ah, of our poor Thames she never heard,
Her foot the Cumner cowslips never stirred.

The coronals of that forgotten time.

And groups under the dreaming garden trees.[1]

The morningless and unawakening sleep.

[1] I might not have recognised these 'groups', but I have a charming edition of the two poems with delightful illustrations by Russell Flint, one of which shows undergraduates talking in New College Garden (or maybe Worcester).

A fugitive and gracious light he seeks,
Shy to illumine; and I seek it too.

And there are even more passages, of four lines to whole stanzas, of flawless beauty, such as the stanza from *The Scholar-Gipsy* beginning 'Still nursing the unconquerable hope', and the complete triad of stanzas from *Thyrsis* beginning, 'So some tempestuous morn in early June'.[1] I found one or two stanzas in the *Gipsy* that just spoilt the 'bright and tranquil' flow, and the twenty-first stanza of *Thyrsis*, about young Daphnis and the Lityerses-song, is too 'allusive' for the non-classically educated reader, but both poems have the pellucid beauty of a Mozart rondo, and their music increases in magical allure with every new reading.

Of the respective merits of the two poems, springing from the same intense memories of Oxford, friendship and rambles through exquisite country, opinion varies from time to time. For long I put the *Gipsy* first, but over the years I have come to rejoice more deeply in *Thyrsis*. Garrod, whose criticism of Arnold was always profound, put *Thyrsis* easily first, and judged Arnold, by the whole temper of his muse, the greatest elegiac poet in our language.[2]

As a postscript to these notes on the two Oxford poems, it may be worth while recalling that of the thirteen poets in the top class between 1500 and 1900 six went to Cambridge (Spenser, Milton, Dryden, Wordsworth, Coleridge and Tennyson) and only two to Oxford (Shelley and Arnold). Between 1900 and 1950 the ratio was reversed (we can no longer confine ourselves to 'poets in the top class'), and in the first half of the present century forty-two poets came out of Oxford and sixteen out of Cambridge. Nevertheless, it is in this period that the only topographically 'Cambridge' poem comparable with our two Oxford ones has been written—Rupert Brooke's sublimely delicious *Grantchester*.

---

[1] Arnold said he himself liked best the stanzas beginning, 'O easy access', 'I know these slopes', 'Where is the girl', 'And long the way appears'.

[2] Mr. Blunden says (*Keats-Shelley Association Bulletin* XII) that in conversation Garrod would set Arnold 'at the head of the Victorian poets'.

CHAPTER V

Of Poetry and Matthew Arnold

SINCE Arnold was admittedly a great critic, we may as well start from his own most celebrated definition. Poetry, he says more than once, is a criticism of life. It is important to notice that in the essay on Joubert he says the aim and end of all literature is criticism of life. This is another matter, and only takes us as far as the point where poetry breaks off from the general term literature to exhibit its own peculiar properties. However, even before we reach this point, poetry is a criticism of life.

Obviously the value and truth of the definition will depend on the meaning of the word 'criticism'. Arnold is nowhere explicit on the meaning he intended. His qualification, 'under the conditions fixed by the laws of poetic truth and poetic beauty', does not really help. Once, as if he were saying the same thing, he declared that 'the noble and profound application of ideas to life is the most essential part of poetic greatness'. This rather suggests the purpose of a good sermon. But the ideas, he says, are in poetry touched with beauty, heightened by emotion. We remember the inadequacy of his definition of religion as morality touched with emotion, and we feel that an idea to which beauty has been added is not good enough. Middleton Murry agreed that poetry was a criticism of life 'just as the beautiful is a criticism of the ugly'. He meant, I suppose, that by its excellence the one shows up the inferiority of the other. But I cannot accept that the purpose of poetry is anything so un-helpful as the showing up of the inferiority of life. When Keats gives us, in the second stanza of the *Ode to Autumn*, that sequence of inimitable images of the spirit of the season—'Who hath not seen thee oft amid thy store?'—he makes us see nature, life, not as something inferior, but as more wonderful than we had thought.

And here we come nearer the point. The better part of criticism is appreciation, and poetry is criticism of life in the sense that it shows us, what few of us have the capacity to see for ourselves, the greatness and beauty and wonder of life. Poetry heightens life. We did not know what England meant to us till we heard Shakespeare speak through John of Gaunt, or the magic of a rose till Tennyson was given one by the Gardener's Daughter. Our senses get dulled by the incidence of living, and the poet comes to interpret life afresh—as Arnold said of Goethe. Elton says that by criticism of life Arnold meant 'something that would illumine and inspire us for the business of living'. But the poet carries the criticism of life further. The critic, as Wilde so brilliantly demonstrated, is an artist, and the poet, the critic of life, not only appreciates and interprets life but creates it. Life itself is the raw material, crude, shapeless, like the marble block from the mountain of the infinite: in the hands of the poet it becomes the lovely and significant thing it was meant to be. The function of the poet is to awaken wonder, the true creative approach to life, by methods that differ from poet to poet.

Synthesising these scattered thoughts, let us venture upon a definition of poetry. Poetry is composition in metrical language which, by its diction and movement, is calculated to give aesthetic pleasure, to heighten appreciation of life, and by stimulating wonder to provide intimations of a greater life beyond. I use the word 'metrical' because I do not believe the full effect of poetry, as expressed in the later parts of the definition, can be achieved in the absence of metre, and I introduce the idea of the 'greater life beyond' (not necessarily 'after') because without some such concept man is a materialist, and poetry cannot come out of materialism.

All that is from the outside. For what goes to the making of poetry, from the soul of the poet into his verse, I will quote from a poet who, with right second to none, looked long and minutely into himself, with this result: 'All lyrical poetry beats with the heart, tells of things seen and felt in a sudden clearness of the senses, and with a flame in the thought. An insatiable delight in life haunts it, and the keen mortal regret that stalks in life's shadow. It springs from a height of living . . . a tension of the spirit, a sense of wonder and mystery, a faith in all that is held most dear, a hope and hunger for an unknown that transcends the known' (from *Behold this Dreamer*, by Walter de la Mare).

Now to apply these criteria to Arnold. The requirements named first in the definition need no arguing: his poetry, by its diction and movement, certainly gives me and many others great aesthetic pleasure (even if at times affronting my mind), and enormously enhances our appreciation of life. The Cumnor hills are more entrancing, the noise of waves on a sea-shore at night is more significant, the thought of eternity more full of 'murmur and scent' for our having read the poems of Matthew Arnold. But does his poetry awaken wonder and so provide intimations of a life beyond our known life? The last clause in the previous sentence gives one affirmative answer, and the vital belief that 'the light we sought is shining still' gives another. Arnold is not steeped in wonder, his poetry does not exist on the verge of a more abundant life, in so full a sense as we feel with Wordsworth, Coleridge, Shelley and Tennyson, but these things are probably truer of him than of Browning, whose passionate love of earthly life resulted in his contacts with the life of the spirit being confined to an occasional experience of what W. O. Raymond calls 'the infinite moment', and though that life can only be known in moments to the common man the poet should have readier and more effective access to the kingdom of light.

Moments of contact with ultimate reality come to Arnold with some frequency. Besides those indicated in the foregoing paragraph, there is the one spoken of in an earlier chapter where he shows, in *The Buried Life*, that he too knows that the peace that comes through love can induce a revelation of the meaning of life, its origin and destiny, completely obscured to ordinary knowledge. Not dissimilar is his realisation, in *A Southern Night*, that beauty of personality links man with the divine substratum of the world. His realisation of a less restricted life is indicated in different images: the thundering River of Life that bore the boat away from desire in *The Dream*, the vision of creation in *In Utrumque Paratus*, those 'far regions of eternal change' seen in *Resignation*, the 'bright procession of eddying forms' that swept through the soul of the *Reveller*, the 'magic of the universe' desired for Urania, the sea's eternal note of sadness, those pure dark regions that had such deep significance on a summer night, the loveliness, magic and grace of nature's youth, the longing like despair of the second *Isolation* poem. And in that Wordsworthian passage already quoted, where he says of his 'lonely heart' that it can only know

> unmating things,
> Ocean and clouds and night and day,
> Lorn autumns and triumphant springs,

there is a strong overtone of transcendence.

Arnold was aware of an 'intangible, unknowable' mode of being encompassing the mortal one; he told Clough that no one had a livelier sense of the 'daemonic element' in human life (one supposes he meant the supernatural, inexplicable). But if he had this sense it makes little impress on his poetry. The signs enumerated above are received with some complacency. The faculty of wonder was not fully developed in Arnold. Generally he is dealing—beautifully and imaginatively—with life at the normal level, and his poetry does not often, like the 'silent form' of the Urn, 'tease us out of thought as doth eternity'.

Perhaps for this reason his genius is not fully recognisable in de la Mare's analysis. Only too often it is the mind arguing, not the heart beating, that we hear. In *Thyrsis* things are seen and felt in 'a sudden clearness of the senses', but not elsewhere. Is there anywhere 'a flame in the thought', such as burns in the briefest lyric of Wordsworth or de la Mare—'*My heart leaps up*' or *Silver*? Yes, it burns in the *Merman* and *Philomela* and not a few of the other poems recently mentioned. Keen mortal regret is very much more obvious than an insatiable delight in life, and little of Arnold's poetry, other than

Thyrsis again, springs from a height of living. I have already said I
find the sense of wonder and mystery fainter than is proper to poetry;
for the faith in all that is held most dear we are constrained to fall
back once more on *Thyrsis*, and the desire for an unknown that
transcends the known rises to a hope and a hunger only in *The
Buried Life*.

These are high demands, and only the great poets fulfil them
much more frequently than Arnold. There are others that he fulfils
adequately. It is the poet's function to illuminate human experience,
and this, in his own domain, he does with complete understanding.
Life is capricious, treating one man generously, another, for no
apparent reason, with persistent cruelty, and for the man to whom
life is an affliction, to read and absorb, to bathe in the melancholy
waters of, such poems as *Dover Beach, Isolation I and II, The Youth of
Man, Obermann I* and *The Grande Chartreuse*, must be a sovereign
salve, like unburdening the heart to a wise and sympathetic confessor.
The appeal to experience is not a necessary one: much poetry lies
far outside experience as commonly known. Kenneth Barnes[1] says
that religion represents our response to the totality of experience;
the poetry of the greatest poets represents their total response to the
whole of experience; a poem is the response—more or less total
according to the stature of the poet—to one particular experience.
Arnold's poetry represents his total response to a very limited
experience, the limitation coming not through circumstances but
from temperament. Mr Eliot complains that Arnold had neither
walked in hell nor been rapt to heaven. One supposes the judgement
is based on conclusions drawn from the poetry, and I should have
thought there was in Arnold's poetry some evidence for at least the
first of these extra-mundane journeys. The second is a much more
rare experience, and few, even of poets, have been worthy, or
capable, of it (most of us are capable, and perhaps worthy, of the
other): this perhaps accounts for the truth—if it is true—of the
assertion that 'our sweetest songs are those that tell of saddest
thought'. I suppose there is no suggestion that the area in between

[1] *The Creative Imagination*, 1960.

hell and heaven—earth, where certainly Arnold did most of his 'walking', and where Milton walked to find *L'Allegro* and *Il Penseroso*—is not deserving of the poet's attention, 'the very world which is the world of all of us', and which, as Wordsworth said, is 'the place in which, in the end, We find our happiness or not at all'.

A limited yet charming and acceptable definition, if not of poetry then of the end of poetry, was given by Mr Day Lewis in his inaugural lecture at Oxford, when he said the poet's task was 'to incline our hearts towards whatever is lovable and admirable in human kind'. This precept perhaps departs from the law that the content of poetry must be not ethical but aesthetic, yet it departs only in the letter. For if morality is defined as the right way of life, and if this is allowed to be the way of beauty and love, then morality can suitably come within the cognizance of poetry. Certainly Arnold's mind, doubtless under the formative influence of his Headmaster-father, was so addicted to morality that he found it impossible (even if he ever tried) to keep it out of his poetry. No other poet has a poem entitled *Morality* (not that the theme is treated unpoetically), and the sense of duty and struggle against inclination is everywhere. (Wordsworth 'wrote the *Ode to Duty* and then had done with that matter'.) Arnold could not be sure that the moral value of a work of art is coextensive with its aesthetic content. *Thyrsis*, and the *Merman*, and the *Reveller* teach us to love beauty, and so inculcate a deeper morality than *Youth's Agitations* or *The World's Triumphs* or *Human Life*, which brood on humanity's shortcomings.

Nor need the content of a poem consist in any large degree of thought, of intellectual activity. Arnold was aware of this, and told Clough that deep thinking was fatal to that more necessary constituent of poetry, sensuousness. Yet he criticised the great romantics for thinking too little, knowing too little, even for reading too little, and himself seems often to make more of reason than of imagination. Perhaps that is why, whereas the key-word of Wordsworth's poetry is joy, that of Arnold's is peace, a precious but negative state, more easily conceived, and on lower levels of the mind. Nevertheless, in the essay on *The Study of Poetry* he suggests that poetry may come to replace religion in interpreting life for us, consoling and sustaining. (I seem to remember that Walter Raleigh made this forecast for humour.) Garrod more advisedly said that poetry is what it is because it answers to a spiritual need in man.

And certainly, though morality, except in its connotation of love and beauty, is generally debarred from poetry, religion in almost any sense, but especially as spiritual awareness, is poetry's twin sister. A narrow moral outlook kills poetry, but even dogmatic religion leaves unimpaired the inspiration of such poems as the *Nativity Ode*, *The Hound of Heaven* and Joseph Mary Plunkett's *I See His Blood upon the Rose*, as well as some well-known hymns. Arnold's poem *Progress*, to which M. Bonnerot draws our attention as a source of knowledge about his religious position, clearly states his belief in the efficacy of the teaching of Christ but stops there, as these other poems do not. All great poets, said Middleton Murry, must be religious, but most poets, great and lesser, have been religious only in the sense—the only necessary sense—of being in vital contact with the universal spirit of life, which in all religions based on the numinous is called God. Arnold is something of a contradiction in this matter. With no fixed beliefs, he yet had a sufficient sense of God, but is unable to let this come through in his poetry, where we have many references to a frustrating 'power' but none to a deity who can be called either transcendent or immanent. In spite of the anthropomorphism of his nature poetry he has no mystic vision of union and communion with nature. As we have seen, only in *The Buried Life* does he admit to having known the mystic moment when one feels in contact with ultimate reality. Nowhere does he seem to share Wordsworth's

> feeling of life endless, the great thought
> By which we live, Infinity and God.

It is part of Arnold's fascination that he is such an enchanting companion through the multi-coloured ways of life. But the supreme poet takes us beyond the here and now, and makes us see, if only in glimpses, the underlying pattern of reality. Life is a shadow of eternity; through the beauty of this world the poet is to show us the eternal beauty. It is indicative of Arnold's refusal or inability to see anything deeply significant in beauty that he seldom uses the word. His poems are full of delectable landscapes, but they are painted for their own sakes—they are as the primrose was to Peter Bell. You may read poem after poem—the *Gipsy*, the *Reveller*, the *Merman*, *The Future*, the *Memorial Verses*, *Resignation* . . . and never light upon the word beauty. It occurs twice in *Thyrsis*, and once (only to be denied) in *Dover Beach*. There is beauty in all the poems named, and Arnold told Clough that the beautiful alone was profoundly poetical, but the idea of beauty is wrapped up with the word, and the idea of beauty—'Beauty, an ideal presence of the earth'—has in itself no power over Arnold.[1] His concentration on the thing to the exclusion of the idea enables him to make the valid distinction between beauty and loveliness. In *Tristram*, Iseult of Brittany is always 'lovely', while beauty is ascribed to the elder Iseult until death comes to give her face 'a tranquil loveliness'. (It is worth noting that beauty is not enough for the modern critic. Mr Eliot says that a poet should see beneath both beauty and ugliness to 'the boredom, the horror and the glory'—and I cannot help admiring the order in which the three necessary perceptions are placed.)

Poetry is not the only source of truth: it is one of the approaches to reality open to the man whose hearing is tuned to art. Arnold presents the appearance and temporalities of the world, human and natural, with power and sympathy, but not so as to set us dreaming of another world to which as yet we have no entry save in dreams. He does not feel the over-riding harmony that subsists between the incongruities of life. There is an affinity between poetry and the mystic experience. This latter is not communicable, and it is the

---

[1] I have not recently read any of the poems of Mr John Masefield (a lesser but true poet), but my most vivid impression of him is of how the idea of beauty, the very word, used to lift him out of and above himself (in the Lollingdon Downs sonnets, for example).

K

virtue of poetry that it can, in some degree, communicate the esoteric knowledge attained by the poet. Every poet is a facet of

> the prophetic soul
> Of the wide world dreaming on things to come.

Garrod believed there was 'a world-consciousness that speaks in poetry'; we may put it more bluntly and say that God speaks through the poet. And here Sir Herbert Read makes the interesting suggestion that since poetry is expressing something that comes from outside himself, the poet's experience and personality are not important. In the matter of personality this may well be true, but for experience we have Rilke's opposing view that 'in order to write one verse one must have had an infinity of experiences'— experiences which, he adds, 'have turned into our blood and ourselves'. The two judgements come out of contrasted philosophies of poetry. The second would rule out Arnold: the first explains why, with his limited experience and pleasingly conventional personality, he was able to produce a few poems of deathless urgency.

If we cannot rank Arnold high among the great imaginative poets it is partly because he himself distrusted imagination—that repetition, as Coleridge called it, in the finite mind of the eternal act of creation— and relied too much upon the finite mind itself and its powerful but limited faculty of reason. Wordsworth said of his poet,

> In common things that round us lie
> Some random truths he can impart:

Arnold would not have admitted that the 'random truths' of a poet might be more illuminating than the cerebrations of a philosopher, any more than he would have accepted the paradox about one impulse from a vernal wood teaching us more than all the sages. There is, however, an interesting sentence in a letter he wrote to a working-man who had sent him an essay: 'a single line of poetry', said the poet-inspector, 'working in the mind, may produce more thought and lead to more light than much "useful knowledge"'. For the parallel to be complete we should have to know what kind of 'line of poetry' he had in mind. He gives no sign that instinct or intuition (that relic, perhaps, of our primitive ancestry) meant much to him. Only in *Thyrsis*, transported by his theme, his memories and the beauty of Thames-side, does he write with the heart of a child and allow the irrational full play. Save here he lacks the element of creative joy: 'While with an eye made quiet by . . . the deep power of joy We see into the life of things'.

It is only through a poet's words and arrangement of words that we can know what it is that he has conceived in his heart. The words of a poem are to the poem itself what appearance is to reality: appearance is all we have to go on in the one case, words are all in the other: interpretation is necessary before we can know what underlies. 'Words, like nature, half-reveal and half-conceal.' It is by love and imagination that we interpret, and the thing is made easier for us if the poet contributes his share of these faculties, if, as Mr Day Lewis says, the poem is 'a love-affair with words'. The essential quality of a poet lies in his use of words: Shakespeare is the supreme poet because of his unequalled mastery of language. Mr Bernard Groom's special studies have led him to the conclusion that Arnold's diction is less interesting than the diction of his great contemporaries, and not often with him does a line, a phrase, a stanza leave us gasping. The excellence of *Dover Beach* lies in the frequency with which this salutary shock occurs. The power of words is enormously enhanced if their arrangement is so moulded by poetic feeling as to result in rhythmic form. Mystical or semi-mystical experience can be conveyed only by words perfectly chosen or by rhythmic form springing from the poet's deep feeling, preferably from a combination of the two. Arnold's poem *The Dream* chronicles one of his rare mystical experiences, and the strange significance of the dream is conveyed largely by the magic of form. In *The Future* the powerful rhythmic movement contributes as much as verbal expression—perhaps more—to the transmission of the vision of life.

In the chapter on art, I tried to show what elements of the classical rule are to be found in Arnold's style. The terms classical and romantic refer equally to the way in which poets conceive their subject, and looked at from this point of view Arnold is today regarded as a traitor to the cause of romanticism, the one who most disastrously let the side down. But once we have agreed that the romantic school of poets at the beginning of the century was greater than the mid-century group, it seems unfair to complain that Arnold's poetry 'declined' from the standard set by Wordsworth and his compeers. The romantic approach, as appears from an analysis of great romantic poetry, is by way of imaginative sensibility achieving profoundest understanding of truth and leading to a removal of the distinction between the natural and the supernatural. The world of sense has for the romantic poet an intense appeal, and from this the aesthetic faculty is stirred to a new consideration of beauty, of the improbable, the intangible, with an awareness of mystery, a flowering of wonder, a realisation of dim openings into the depth of things. Romantic poetry, says Grierson, is 'shot through with new and strange beauties of thought and vision'. And the root, as also the bloom, of the process is a special intimacy with and understanding of nature.

Now this does not in any very full sense suggest Arnold. He is a great nature poet, but only in *The Scholar-Gipsy* does nature mean more to him than a response of intense pleasure, while beauty, we have seen, does not stir him to a special depth of awareness, because, as Elton says, he 'does not abandon himself to beauty.' The terms 'improbable, intangible, mystery, wonder,' have little relevance for the content of Arnold's poetry, and though his beauties are copious they are seldom 'new and strange'. The appeal of the senses is felt only in his love of colour in flowers and in the sounds that give brilliance to *Dover Beach*. Only once or twice, in *A Dream*, *The Voice*, do we feel the natural flowing over into the supernatural. Generally Arnold did not share the romantic belief that imagination, the aesthetic sense, was the gateway to true knowledge, but imaginative sensibility underlies the great vision of *The Future*. And in the two Oxford poems, as also in the conclusion to *Sohrab and Rustum*, all the elements of romantic poetry may be found, including the one which is almost absent from the bulk of Arnold's poetry, the sense of mystery and wonder. On the other hand, the stoical ideal that is the soul of the classical way of life is present, in a form sometimes more complete and sometimes less, in much of Arnold's poetry, notably in *Resignation*, *Empedocles*, *Self-Dependence* and *Morality*. The Greek serenity that he admired in Sophocles and longed for in his own life, but which he found overwhelmed by the feverish activity of the modern world, got itself expressed more often in his style than in his thought, where, however, there is always a classical balance of imagination by reason.

Arnold has been variously described as the poet of intimacy, of strife, of feeling, of intellect. These last two must always be there, but are only truly successful if present in a peculiar poetical blend which Wordsworth called 'feeling intellect': that is, intellect, the mind, used like an instrument for cutting down to the truth, but used with its feeling edge rather than with its rational—which was generally the one employed by Arnold. 'Feeling intellect' is perhaps imagination, and the great romantics believed in 'imagination teaching truth', though, as D. G. James points out, their imagination led not to philosophy but to vision, and truth was revealed in 'the spectacle of life'. This is an aspect of the subtler faculty of intuition, about which Arnold did not know much. He could rarely be completely objective and concrete: his own self was always in the way. This accounts for the 'intimacy' and also perhaps for the 'strife'. There was nothing in him of the 'poetical character' Keats recognised as having 'no self . . . no character . . . no Identity'. He falls in better with Coleridge's demand that a poet should have an 'androgynous mind'. A deficiency is that he does not seem to know 'the self-sufficing power of solitude'. He complains of the fate that has ordained loneliness for man. When distracted by the problem of his relations with Marguerite he implores the mountains to let him retire to their unpeopled slopes, but there is no indication that he went, or that 'impulses of deeper birth' ever came to him in solitude: once perhaps, in *A Summer Night*; and he at least recommended the Gipsy to continue his solitary wanderings.

If Spenser is the poet's poet, Arnold is the literary man's poet: he has no attributes that could give him popular appeal. In his lifetime the dull academic critic judged him 'a graceful versifier, lacking the energy and fire of the great poet', but Swinburne, reviewing the 1867 volume, praised it for majesty and composure of thought, perfect clearness and competence in the verse. George Eliot said that he 'grew upon her' more than other poets, which is how I feel about him. He was his own severest critic. 'My poems have weight, I think, but no charm'. That last is certainly not true. We may argue about the genuine weight of the poetic substance, but the charm—intimate, melancholy, unambiguous—is inescapable. When he said, 'My poems, viewed absolutely, are little or nothing', he was making a judgement that cannot so easily be put aside. How many poems by how many poets are worth much when 'viewed absolutely'? But I will venture to assert some degree of absolute greatness for *Thyrsis* and *The Scholar-Gipsy*, *Tristram and Isolde* and *The Forsaken Merman*, the second *Isolation* poem to Marguerite, *Philomela*, *Dover Beach* and *The Future*, *A Summer Night*, the *Memorial Verses*, and perhaps *Urania*, *Requiescat*, *Sohrab and Rustum* and *A Dream*.

(The reader may be relieved to know that this is the last mention of *A Dream*. I do not apologise for the frequency of the references—I have counted them and believe there are ten—but will suggest that you, the querulous reader, turn up the poem and see if you do not agree with me about the moving quality of its theme and the flawless art of its composition.)

I began by saying that I find Matthew Arnold a poet of great delight, and I have repeated this at intervals throughout the book. But in the main I have been pulling the flower to pieces and botanising, not always enthusiastically, on the petals. Yet the flower comes together again, all colour and perfume, and is as delightful as ever. Since writing the preceding paragraph I have read again the poems named therein—for a poet, like a man, should be judged by his best—and a number of others too, and have got, over and over again, the authentic feel of great poetry. If the divine despair that great art can awaken comes only with an occasional line, it comes then unmistakably—'He could not wait their passing, he is dead'. If there is not often the rich verbal texture that clothes the thought of the supreme poets, beauty of a plainer kind is seldom absent, form and style are always there, and the strings of the heart are lightly touched to music, the music of Chopin if not the music of Mozart. It has been said that poetry will not save the soul but may make it worth saving, and Arnold's poetry very surely is capable of this blessed effect. For years I have carried a pocket volume of his poems, and to walk over the downs making distressful love with Matthew and Marguerite, to sit beside the sea and share the anguish of Tristram, to move majestically with Oxus and the River of Time while riding on the top-deck of a country bus—to do these things has lifted me, for the moment, a little nearer heaven.

I have not seen reason to alter my placing of Arnold as third, and a good third, among the poets belonging to the period 1830-1890. Only prejudice can fail to see him over-shadowed by Tennyson and Browning, but he is not dwarfed in their company. And though there is a good deal of competition for that third place— Elizabeth Browning, Clough, Patmore, Meredith and Hardy, the two Rossettis, Morris, Swinburne, Hopkins, Henley and Stevenson —and although some of these poets wrote one or more poems as good as Arnold's best, none of them can show a mass of enduring verse comparable with his.

His special combination of intimacy of feeling with classical form arouses in some good elder critics a personal enthusiasm that may over-rule the standards of pure criticism. His music is generally in an attractive minor key: his tunes, like his moods, have an acid flavour that keeps them from cloying as sweeter melodies may. If mid-century critics can accept him as a poet the gain will be theirs as well as his.

Partial Bibliography

(Books to which reference is made in the text, and others consulted)

A

The Poetical Works of Matthew Arnold, ed. Tinker and Lowry. Oxford University Press, 1950.

The Poetry of Matthew Arnold: a Commentary, by Tinker and Lowry. Oxford University Press, 1940.

Matthew Arnold, a Selection, ed. Kenneth Allott. Penguin Books, 1961.

The Letters of Matthew Arnold, 1848-1888, collected by G. W. E. Russell, 1900.

The Letters of Matthew Arnold to A. H. Clough, ed. H. F. Lowry, 1932.

Letters from Matthew Arnold to Robert Browning, contributed by John Drinkwater, *Cornhill*, Dec. 1923.

Matthew Arnold's Notebooks, ed. Lowry, Young and Dunn, 1952.

B

Swinburne, *Essays and Studies*. 1875.

Saintsbury, *Matthew Arnold*. 1899.

G. W. E. Russell, *Matthew Arnold*. 1904.

Oliver Elton, *Tennyson and Matthew Arnold*. 1924.

E. K. Chambers, *Matthew Arnold*. 1932, 1947.

H. Kingsmill, *Matthew Arnold*. 1928.

H. W. Garrod, *Poetry and the Criticism of Life*. 1931.

L. Bonnerot, *Matthew Arnold, Poète*. 1947.

J. D. Jump, *Matthew Arnold*. 1950.

Isobel Macdonald, *The Buried Self*.

L. Trilling, *Matthew Arnold*. 1949.

Edmund Blunden, *Matthew Arnold*, in *The Great Victorians*, ed. Massingham.

D. G. James, *Matthew Arnold and the Decline of English Romanticism.* 1961.

A. Harris, *Matthew Arnold, the Unknown Years.* (*Nineteenth Century*, April 1933.)

J. M. Murry, *Matthew Arnold Today.* (*Times Literary Supplement*, April 6, 1946.)

C

Garrod, *The Profession of Poetry.* 1928.

Raleigh, *Style.*

Saintsbury, *History of Prosody.*

Ideas and Beliefs of the Victorians (B.B.C. talks).

Helen Gardner, *The Business of Criticism.* 1959.

H. W. Nevinson, *Visions and Memories.* 1944.

R. A. Foakes, *The Romantic Assertion.* 1960.

T. S. Eliot, *The Use of Poetry and the Use of Criticism.* 1933.

Herbert Read, *Form in Modern Poetry.* 1952.

N. Wymer, *Arnold of Rugby.* 1953.

T. W. Bamford, *Thomas Arnold.* 1960.

Basil Willey, *Nineteenth Century Studies.* 1949.

F. W. Bateson, *English Poetry and the English Language.*

G. H. Ford, *Keats and the Victorians.* 1945.

Bernard Groom, *Poetic Diction from Spenser to Bridges.* 1955.

G. M. Young, *Victorian England.* 1936.

(Katherine Chorley, *Arthur Hugh Clough: The Uncommitted Mind*, appeared too late to be of use.)

Index